Date Due

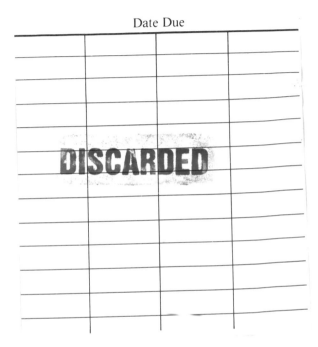

DISCOVERING
the
PLAIN
TRUTH

How the
Worldwide Church of God
Encountered
the Gospel of Grace

LARRY NICHOLS
& GEORGE MATHER

InterVarsity Press
Downers Grove, Illinois

InterVarsity Press
P.O. Box 1400, Downers Grove, IL 60515
World Wide Web: www.ivpress.com
E-mail: mail@ivpress.com

*InterVarsity Press® is the book-publishing division of InterVarsity Christian Fellowship/USA®, a
student movement active on campus at hundreds of universities, colleges and schools of nursing in the
United States of America, and a member movement of the International Fellowship of Evangelical
Students. For information about local and regional activities, write Public Relations Dept.,
InterVarsity Christian Fellowship/USA, 6400 Schroeder Rd., P.O. Box 7895, Madison, WI 53707-7895.*

Cover art courtesy of Plain Truth Ministries Worldwide

ISBN 0-8308-1969-X

Printed in the United States of America ♻

Library of Congress Cataloging-in-Publication Data
Nichols, Larry A.
    *Discovering the plain truth : how the Worldwide Church of God encountered the gospel
of grace / Larry Nichols & George Mather.*
        p.   cm.
    Includes bibliographical references.
    ISBN 0-8308-1969-X (alk. paper)
    *1. Worldwide Church of God—History.   2. Worldwide Church of God—Doctrines.   I. Mather,
George A.   II. Title.*
BX6178.N53   1998
289.9—dc21   *97-43047*
                                                                                                        CIP

19	18	17	16	15	14	13	12	11	10	9	8	7	6	5	4	3	2	1
14	13	12	11	10	09	08	07	06	05	04	03	02	01	00	99	98		

For Zelia, my soulmate,
whose twenty-one wonderful years
of love and devotion
are a gift from God.
Her patience with me made it possible
for me to continue to write.
I also dedicate this book to
my four wonderful daughters,
whose names we based on four
words from the Greek New Testament:
Melissa (sweet as honey),
Charissa (grace), Alicia (truth)
and Faythe (faith, of course).
LN

To the two women I adore most.
First my wife, Sharon, who has shared my hurts
and disappointments and through it all
has provided happiness for over thirty years
She is my "Rose of Sharon,"
and in comparison with her,
all others are brambles (Song 2:1).
Second, my daughter, Jennifer, who helped to teach me
that a husband is the head of his wife so far as he is
to her what our blessed Savior is to the church.
He is to love her as Christ loved the church
and to give his life for her (Eph 5:25).
GM

Preface   *9*

Acknowledgments   *12*

1 Forgive Us Our Trespasses   *13*

2 How It All Began   *18*

3 Anatomy of a Cult   *41*

4 A Modern-Day Reformation?   *60*

5 Reactions   *72*

6 From the Outside Looking In   *83*

Appendix 1: Doctrinal Changes in the
        WCG Since 1986   *91*

Appendix 2: Interview 1   *100*

Appendix 3: Interview 2   *120*

Notes   *133*

Bibliography   *139*

Preface

My first encounter with the Worldwide Church of God was through a radio broadcast. I (Larry Nichols) was thirteen years old at the time, and I distinctly remember working on a model clipper ship in my basement with the radio on as a charismatic voice spoke about the true understanding of the Bible and *The Plain Truth* magazine. I became a little excited and found myself actually listening, something I did not do very well on Sunday mornings when I was shuffled off to church. I was impressed with the way Scripture passages were quoted with precision. (What did a young teenager really know about precision? I was having enough trouble trying to build that model ship.) As I listened, I was even more impressed that I could order *The Plain Truth* and it would be sent free of charge.

My first copy arrived several weeks later, and I began reading with avid interest. I recall being fascinated with the way the magazine's various authors were able to weave in Bible passages with current events, making the Bible seem relevant to today. A short, gray-haired man was pictured on many of its pages, seated at a desk, standing at a podium or shaking hands with foreign heads of state and dignitaries. I said to myself, *Who is this guy? He must be rather important.*

As it happened, despite my early interest in *The Plain Truth,* I drifted away from things religious and spiritual in my teen years. Nevertheless, years later I found myself enrolled at Concordia Theological Seminary, ready to complete theological studies for ordination into the

holy ministry in the Lutheran Church Missouri Synod. At Concordia
I met George Mather, another seminary student with a loud green
Boston Celtic jacket and a Boston brogue thicker than that of the Celtic
great Bob Cousy. A friendship ensued between George and his wife
Sharon and my wife Zelia and me, as well as our children. I quickly
learned that George had an extensive collection of files and data on
religious cults and the occult which he had amassed from many years'
work for Christian Research Institute under the late Walter Martin.
From our friendship came our first book, *Dictionary of Cults, Sects,
Religions and the Occult* (1993). One of the groups covered there was
the Worldwide Church of God (WCG). And now we have had an
opportunity to work together on these topics again.

The plan of this book is rather straightforward. Chapter one considers briefly the present situation and spells out briefly what has taken
place that has made the telling of this story both possible and necessary.
Chapter two recounts a brief history of the life of Herbert W. Armstrong
and the WCG up until 1986, the year of his death. The next chapter
explores Armstrong's teachings and beliefs. Here we also offer a
definition of the word *cult* and the reasons we believe that the WCG
under the leadership of Armstrong was indeed deserving of that label.

Chapter four picks up the story from 1986 to the present. The years
from 1986 to 1997 are known as the Tkach era, as Joseph Sr. and Joseph
Jr., father and son, have been at the helm as pastors general of the WCG
during this time. We present the changes that have taken place from
their perspectives and explain where they see the WCG heading in the
future.

The next chapter takes a different turn. Whenever anything significant
comes to public attention, there are reactions, both favorable and unfavorable. Some have reacted positively to the WCG changes and have concluded that they are tantamount to a modern-day Reformation. Others,
however, have concluded that there is really little reason to rejoice. By
attempting to include both perspectives, our book provides balance that
will allow our readers to decide whether the WCG continues to be a "cult
of Christianity" or has become a denomination within the fold of Protestant Christendom.

In the last chapter we ponder what the future holds for the WCG and add some observations and reflections. Appendix one summarizes the changes in WCG doctrine since 1986 and includes some of our reflections on these changes. In this past year George Mather has conducted two interviews with Joseph Tkach Jr. and two other key leaders in the WCG, Mike Feazell and Gregory Albrecht. The first interview was taped and transcribed and is found in appendix two. The second interview was a personal meeting among the same four individuals, followed by a written response to the questions posed by George at the interview. These responses are found in appendix three. We both visited the leaders for a third meeting, which was casual, with no taping and very little note taking. It was also the longest meeting, as Tkach and Albrecht hosted George and me for almost four hours. There are numerous references to this meeting throughout the book.

We recognize that though we have tried to give a fair account of the WCG's changes, we have not included every perspective. This has not been possible. Whole chapters could have been added to cover the points of view of current salaried ministers, lay pastors and pastors who have resigned but have remained members of the WCG. Perhaps such perspectives will be addressed in a future edition, or a separate work altogether.

Many years have passed since that day I first heard about the WCG. My interest in building clipper ships has long since waned, but the study of religions has become both a passion and a profession for me. So I find myself, with George, writing a book about the first religious group that ever really interested me. We recount the WCG's history and explore its claim to have made a transition away from former teachings and its current quest to place itself theologically within the mainstream of historic orthodox Christianity.

Acknowledgments

Many people are due our thanks for helping make this book possible. They include the present leaders of the Worldwide Church of God— Pastor General Joseph Tkach Jr., Gregory Albrecht and Michael Feazell—for being most gracious, hospitable and cooperative, especially when we asked hard and imposing questions. David Covington is to be thanked for his many contributions via the Internet and telephone interviews, and Earl Williams is also gratefully acknowledged for telling us his side of the story. Tom Lapaka, William Meyer, Mark Tabladillo and William Ferguson added much with their insights and mailings over the Internet. Andrew Le Peau of InterVarsity Press, our editor, made suggestions along the way that proved extremely helpful.

We would like to thank their families as well. George acknowledges his wife, Sharon, and his children, Jennifer, Christian, Joshua and Andrew. Larry acknowledges and thanks his wife, Zelia, and daughters Melissa, Charissa, Alicia and Faythe. All our family members gave up many hours with us so that we could continue to write this book. The following are to be thanked for their critical reading of the manuscript: Dr. Theodore P. Letis, Tom and Linda Lapaka, Melissa Nichols and David Covington. Also, special thanks to Charissa Nichols for her diligence at the copy machine. I (Larry) would like to offer a special acknowledgment, in the year of his retirement, to Dr. Calvin Hoslinger, who inspired my interest in history.

ONE

Forgive Us
Our Trespasses

American history is truly remarkable.
Let's talk about it.
LARRY NELSON

*O*ver the years the Worldwide Church of God has enjoyed
renown far out of proportion to its size. Its magazine, *The Plain Truth*,
has had a circulation of over six million even though baptized membership in the church never reached one hundred thousand. The
church's well-known radio and later its television program, both called
The World Tomorrow, hosted by WCG founder Herbert W. Armstrong,
were heard by millions of others around the world.

Yet the WCG was considered by many to be a cult because of its
unorthodox doctrines. It strongly denied the Trinity, denied that Jesus
was human and denied that the soul was immortal; at the same time it
held dogmatically to many Old Testament practices and idiosyncratic
beliefs. (Chapter three addresses its teachings in more depth.)

The March/April 1996 issue of *The Plain Truth* carried an article
by Pastor General Joseph Tkach Jr., the current head of the WCG,
stating that the church was retreating from its previous unorthodox

beliefs and practices and moving toward the gospel of grace. The article, entitled "Forgive Us Our Trespasses," included the following statements:

> The Worldwide Church of God, sponsor of *The Plain Truth*, has changed its position on numerous long-held beliefs and practices during the past few years. At the heart of those changes has been an acceptance that salvation is by grace through faith. . . .
>
> For decades we regarded scrupulous adherence to the law as the basis of our righteousness. We attempted to relate to God through old covenant rules and regulations in our fervent desire to please him. . . .
>
> We were judgmental and self righteous, condemning other Christians. . . . We imposed on our members a works-oriented approach to Christian living. . . . We've been wrong. There was never an intent to mislead anyone. . . . We make no attempt to cover up the doctrinal and scriptural errors of our past. . . .
>
> So we stand today at the foot of the cross—the ultimate symbol of all reconciliation. . . . We desire to meet there with anyone we may have injured.
>
> It is only by the blood of the lamb and the power of the Spirit that we can put the hurts of the past behind us and move forward to our common goal.
>
> So to all members, former members, co-workers and others . . . I extend my sincerest heartfelt apologies. And I invite you to join us in proclaiming the true gospel of Jesus Christ around the world.[1]

What factors led to this remarkable statement? How have Armstrong's teachings actually been changed? How have the changes affected the membership of the church today? Is the publisher of *The Plain Truth* now preaching "the plain truth" concerning the life, death and resurrection of Jesus Christ?

The answers to these questions form the story we tell in this book. Our work presents the exciting account of the WCG, its rise, stunning growth, remarkable successes, failures and significant changes, all in the interest of "discovering the plain truth."

As cult specialists, we have written about the Worldwide Church of God (WCG), popularly known as Armstrongism, before. But over the last eleven years it seems that almost every aspect of this church founded by Armstrong has changed.

Discovering the Plain Truth is not the story of any one person's pilgrimage from cult to Christianity, but rather the story of the WCG and its transition as church body from the unorthodox teachings of Herbert W. Armstrong to an evangelical form of traditional Christianity. If these changes are in fact genuine, and if the WCG has indeed become a Protestant denomination in the traditional sense, then indeed the changes are almost without precedent in church history. It is extremely rare for whole groups to make a transition to orthodoxy.[2]

This book is the result of our in-depth investigation of the church, which included several personal interviews with top WCG officials, discussions with former WCG members, and involvement in ongoing dialogues between WCG leaders and the Christian community.

Changes and Challenges

The day of our last visit with WCG leaders before completing this book, our automobile made its way east on busy Freeway 134 to the Pasadena exit onto Orange Grove Boulevard. It was a beautiful cloudless, sunny day, typical of southern California. We immediately spotted a striking complex of buildings to the left side of the boulevard. An elegant sign on the velvety lawn informed us that we had arrived at the headquarters of the Worldwide Church of God.

We were eager to meet with Pastor General Joseph Tkach Jr., the leader of an organization that was announcing to the world that it had renounced many of the teachings of the founder of the WCG, Herbert W. Armstrong.

Being a little early for our appointment, we walked around the lobby where visitors are welcomed. Glass cases held an ostentatious display of treasures that Armstrong and his successor, the late Joseph Tkach Sr., had amassed over the years from foreign dignitaries. Among them were a golden replica of the *Mayflower,* a golden peacock from Queen Sirikit of Thailand, a silver fig tree from Syria, beautiful menorah candles, a vase from Prince Takabiti of Japan, a carriage clock from England, bagpipes from Scotland, a Viking dragon ship from Norway and, closer to home, a crystal automobile from Detroit. But these impressive items were tokens of a bygone era. They serve only as reminders of a time that is no more.

We were soon greeted by a pleasant secretary and ushered into the pastor general's office. After warm handshakes and an exchange of pleasantries, we found ourselves sitting with the man who had asked for so many to "forgive us . . ." His office was as much a memorial to more opulent times as was the vestibule downstairs, with an oak desk, a round conference table, handsome bookshelves, and many family photos. Apologetically, Tkach volunteered that such elegant luxury was the way of Herbert W. Armstrong. Plans were in the making, he said, to reconstruct the office and give it a much more unassuming appearance.

But given the more significant developments that have already taken place at the very core of the WCG, and all they imply for the church's future, changes in decor will be the least of Tkach's worries in the years ahead. His article in *The Plain Truth* was an extended plea for the forgiveness of past transgressions. It was his attempt to reach out to many who were hurting and whose lives were harmed by both the teaching and the practice of the WCG over the years. Tkach's hope is, he told us, that these ex-members might find it in their hearts to forgive.

For many of them, reconciliation has not been possible. Here is the testimony of one family from Iowa who spent over twenty-two years in the WCG and left in 1995:

> Some of the struggles we faced were 1) isolation, 2) re-entering our culture and community, 3) facing the feelings of being used and betrayed by a group to which we gave our lives, 4) knowing harm came to our children's relationship with God from having been part of a cult (and not knowing exactly how to help them now), and 5) dealing with feelings of being robbed spiritually, emotionally, and financially.
>
> Most helpful has been 1) our faith in Christ—that he led us out of the WCG and that He is lovingly guiding our healing process, 2) knowledge of what dysfunctionality is and how it is reflected in cults . . .[3]

Similar stories abound. During our conversation with Joe Tkach and Greg Albrecht that morning and on into the afternoon, they said they

werc painfully aware of the difficult recovery faced by many cx-mcm-
bers. They spoke of the pain that they themselves have undergone. With
so many changes, membership in the WCG has dropped drastically.[4]
Tkach and Albrecht told us that some ex-members have even written
nasty and threatening letters.

Embracing Grace

During our time in Pasadena we were able to take up a number of
theological matters with Albrecht and Tkach, such as baptism, the
Lord's Supper, the church and other doctrines. The word *grace* came
up quite often. Both leaders said they understood grace to mean the
unmerited favor and mercy of God given to the world in and through
the sacrifice of Jesus Christ. They spoke of coming to know such grace
for themselves and lamented that grace had been missing from a
religion that had been built upon the very opposite—law. They said
that the WCG leadership has been relearning theology based on New
Testament teachings and that grace is the key doctrine needed to
rebuild and to heal not only their own lives but also the lives of many
who have been wounded and have left the WCG.

From our interviews with the WCG leadership and with many
ex-members, it is clear that many have been discovering the grace of
God in Jesus Christ. Yet the wounds of the past seem so deep that
distrust and hurt continue to keep grace-filled forgiveness and healing
from taking place between those who believe similarly in many
respects but have chosen to go their separate ways.

At the beginning of this chapter we noted that millions of people
have heard of Herbert W. Armstrong and Armstrongism. But we
suspect that many more people are not aware of the "trespasses" for
which the new pastor general has been seeking forgiveness on behalf
of the WCG. Those trespasses are a central part of this fascinating story.
To them we now turn our attention.

TWO

How It
All Began

*The reader is reminded that I had chosen,
instead of the university,
the process of self-education,
selecting my own courses of study.*

HERBERT W. ARMSTRONG,

AUTOBIOGRAPHY

*I*n 1929 the stock market was about to collapse and send the United States into the worst economic crisis in its short history. The Great Depression took place during the administration of President Herbert Hoover. And in the late 1920s another Herbert, having already undergone three business failures himself in his young life, would experience a change that would put him on a course of ascendancy to a different presidency—that of a church. The avid followers of Herbert W. Armstrong would soon come to believe that the importance of his role far outweighed in importance that of a mere president of a great nation. For this Herbert, a divinely appointed call would launch him on a career that would grant him audiences with heads of state and dignitaries the world over.

Much of what Armstrong wanted people to know about him is found in his autobiography and in other writings, particularly *The Plain Truth* magazine, which often quoted many of his statements throughout his long life. He writes of his past, his childhood, the beginning of his ministry, relationships with his wife and children, and the leadership of the WCG. Aside from the issue of memory when a person is recounting events from his early life years later, any historian would encounter problems with autobiographical sources such as this. Given what Armstrong believed about himself, that he was called by God to be the leader of the WCG, the one true church, much of his writing is consumed with his sense of importance.

A Sense of Destiny

A student enrolled in a Methodist seminary receives a Methodist doctrine and teaching into his head. A Catholic student studying in a Catholic seminary is taught Roman Catholic teachings. A student in a Presbyterian seminary is given Presbyterian doctrines. A student in Germany studying history is instructed in one version of World Wars I and II, but a history student in the United States is taught a somewhat different version.

But I had been called specially by the living God.[1]

These words, written late in Armstrong's life, explain why in at least some instances he interpreted the events of his birth and earlier days in ways that cannot be reconciled with the facts. For example, given that he embraced Anglo-Israelism (the belief that England and then America constitute the lost ten tribes of Israel— examined in chapter three) as an official WCG doctrine, he had an interest in noting, in the 1957 version of his autobiography, that he had genealogical records linking him to Edward I of England. From there he traces his ancestry "through the British Royal genealogy back to King Herremon of Ireland who married Queen Tea Tephi, the daughter of Zedekiah, the Queen of Judah."[2] Armstrong offers no documentation to substantiate this claim. The last book Armstrong ever wrote, *Mystery of the Ages,* says it this way:

I have my genealogy all the way back to Edward the First of England and a line extending back to King David of ancient Israel. I have been astonished to discover this genealogy and the fact that I am, on one side of my family, actually of "the house of David." My forebears emigrated from England to Pennsylvania with William

Penn, a hundred years before the United States became a nation.[3] Once a prospective employer turned him down for work because there were no openings, and Armstrong responded, "Do you realize that you probably don't get a chance once in several years to add a man of my caliber, my talents, and ambition and *will* to work!"[4] Such self-assurance would be the outstanding quality that would enable Armstrong to persevere and eventually succeed in building the WCG.[5]

Beginnings

Herbert W. Armstrong was born on July 31, 1892, to Horace and Eva Armstrong, a Quaker couple then living in Des Moines, Iowa. His father did not hold a steady job throughout Herbert's early childhood. Before he was twelve years old, the family had moved six times. One of these moves was to Marshalltown, Iowa. Here his father became part owner of a flour mill. Other moves were to Union, Iowa, then back to Des Moines, where Horace Armstrong tried to manufacture and market an innovative type of furnace.

Herbert Armstrong later claimed that his mother was "something like a third cousin" to President Herbert Hoover. Young Armstrong had a sister named Mabel, two years his junior, who died at the age of nine, a brother eight years younger, and a brother and sister (twins) twelve years younger. The youngest brother, Dwight Leslie, would prove a gifted hymn writer.

Herbert was not an exceptional child in any way during his growing-up years. He participated in a number of sports, including ice-skating, track, wrestling, football, and baseball. He did not excel in any of these, nor were his academic achievements noteworthy. Armstrong recalls in his autobiography that he spent considerable time reading the Greek philosophers Plato, Aristotle and Epictetus. When he began dating, he would lose interest rather quickly in a girl who could not converse with him about philosophy or other intellectual matters.

Armstrong considered going to college but decided against it for at least two reasons. A vocational analysis test suggested that he possessed the gifts necessary to succeed in advertising, and his uncle Frank encouraged him to avoid college and seek employment with a Des Moines newspaper called the *Daily Capital.*

Herbert quit high school at the end of his sophomore year. His lack of a formal education, however, did not prevent him from putting his gifts to work. His ambitions enabled him to succeed in advertising despite some setbacks and failures. He would later view these years as preparatory for what God was planning to carry out in his life.

Guided by his uncle, young Herbert spent hours reading literature and instruction guides on sales and advertising. His communication skills improved rapidly. Soon he received a promotion, and his salary was raised to eight dollars per week—even by the standards of the 1920s hardly enough to support himself. So he pressed on.

At the age of nineteen, Armstrong learned about a job opportunity that would take him far from home. He became a paymaster at a sawmill in Wiggins, Mississippi. This experience did not prove to be pleasant. After six months he was hospitalized with typhoid fever. Upon regaining his health, Herbert returned to Des Moines and went to work for *The Merchant's Trade Journal,* where he remained for the next three years. Here he was responsible for writing and conducting research in order to come up with new ideas for interesting articles that would promote the publication. This required a considerable amount of traveling to poll businesses and government agencies. Armstrong apparently later believed that this interviewing experience had made him a pioneer in public opinion polls.[6]

After three years, the quality of his work began to wane. Receiving a strongly worded letter from his home office, Armstrong became convinced that he was going to be fired. Rather than suffer the indignity of it, he explains, "I had to 'beat them to it,' by resigning, avoiding the stigma of being discharged."[7] When he returned to Des Moines, he discovered that his boss had had no intention of letting him go.

Armstrong subsequently applied his sales skills to a variety of other product lines, including motor club memberships and pianos. He himself enjoyed playing the piano, but he reports that during his tenure with the Benjamin Piano Company, which lasted for two months at the most, he did not sell a single instrument.

The impulse to travel, perhaps fostered by the many moves his family made in his formative years, was virtually a part of Armstrong's constitution. It would remain his habit throughout his life. After the piano venture, he moved back to Iowa and went to work for a trade journal called *Northwest Banker.* His responsibility was selling advertising for new bank buildings in the state.

Relative success in this business brought him to Chicago, where he opened an office as a publisher's agent. Some innovative ideas relating to the advertising of farm equipment in bank journals netted him a substantial raise in pay. But this success was tempered by his inability to work smoothly with other people. What could have proved a very profitable enterprise thus yielded him only enough income to get by in the circles of bankers and other wealthy people.

During his seven-year tenure in Chicago, Armstrong made regular trips back to Des Moines. On one of those trips he met and fell in love with a third cousin, Loma Dillon. He described her as "that innocent, completely unspoiled freshness of a breath of spring."[8] They were married on Herbert's birthday, July 31, 1917, by a minister at Oak Park Baptist Church in Chicago. During the first three years of their marriage, Herbert's business prospered. They became the parents of two daughters, Beverly Lucille and Dorothy Jane.

The year 1920 proved to be a watershed, as a depression hit and Armstrong experienced a reversal of fortune. The advertising business declined, and Armstrong's business went broke. He struggled for the next two years to keep the business afloat, but his losses far outweighed his gains. Sending Loma and the children back to Iowa, he remained in Chicago to attempt to rebuild on his own. But for the next three months Armstrong overindulged in alcohol with two other advertising men, frequenting cabarets late into the night.[9]

Suddenly he decided he had had enough. Quitting Chicago, he returned to Iowa and went to work on his father-in-law's farm. He gained a meager income at this time from some small advertising sales.

Loma Armstrong would prove an extremely influential part of her husband's life. After three years of farm work in Iowa, she suggested that they move to Salem, Oregon, where Herbert's parents had moved twelve years before. Loma's parents also accompanied them, and together they moved west in the summer of 1924.

In Salem, Herbert continued to do what he knew best: selling. He worked in several advertising ventures, including a Vancouver, Washington, newspaper called the *Columbian.* He remained in Vancouver for six months, after which he moved back to Salem, where he entered a partnership in the laundry detergent business. This also brought another setback, despite Armstrong's hopes that it would be his most successful venture yet. From 1925 through 1933 the Armstrongs struggled, like many others during the Great Depression, as Herbert was barely able to make ends meet from the odd jobs that he managed to get, including door-to-door sales.

Marion McNair, a former staff member of the WCG, now a sharp critic of Armstrong, summarizes the final phase of Armstrong's secular advertising career thus:

> His final try at advertising was in late 1931. He decided to take a job with *The Messenger,* a local newspaper in Astoria, Oregon. It was on its last leg when he came aboard and in February 1933, as if symbolic of Armstrong's total career, *The Messenger* collapsed as Armstrong walked away from it. Armstrong had a newfound sanctuary—that of religion.[10]

Religious Evolution

By 1931 Armstrong had already been reading the Bible for several years. Loma had befriended an elderly neighbor named Ora Runcorn in Salem in 1925. Mrs. Runcorn was a student of the Bible and involved Loma in Bible studies. The Armstrongs had been members of the Methodist denomination since their days in Chicago.

Actually, religion had been important to the Armstrongs, at least to Loma, from the outset of their marriage. Just a few days after they made their vows, Loma had reported having had a dream in which she saw angels descending with the message that Jesus was returning soon. Herbert recalls being embarrassed the morning Loma told him of her vision. He said that he responded like Jonah, running away from what he later came to believe was a message from God. "God dealt with me in no uncertain terms, even as he had dealt with Moses, Isaiah, Jeremiah, Jonah, Andrew, Peter, and the Apostle Paul."[11] Armstrong referred to Loma's dream as "the unrecognized call."

The key insight Loma adopted from Mrs. Runcorn was the convic- tion that Saturday, the Jewish sabbath, was the correct day of the week for worship. She eagerly brought her new insight to her husband. At this point, some seven years after the dream, Herbert still did not share her enthusiasm for religion. He was actually quite angered by what he concluded was fanaticism. Their relationship became strained to the point of near divorce. Before it came to that, however, Herbert agreed in the fall of 1926, at the age of thirty-four, to take up his wife's offer to surrender her belief in the Saturday sabbath if he could prove her wrong. Turning to the Bible with an angry zeal, Armstrong determined to study this doctrine.

Then Armstrong's sister-in-law, Hertha Dillon, presented him with another challenge. "Herbert Armstrong," she accused contemptuously, "you are just plain ignorant! Everybody who has any education knows human life has come by evolution!"[12] Armstrong wrote in his *Autobiography* years later:

Her words stabbed deeply into what was left of my ego. One is uneducated and ignorant unless he believes in evolution. All educated people now believe it. That accusation came hot on the heels of this Sabbath challenge from my wife. . . . "Hertha," I responded, "I am just starting a study of the Bible. I intend to include in this research a thorough study of the Biblical account of creation . . . and I will include an in-depth study of evolution. I feel sure that a thorough study into both sides will show that it is *you* who are ignorant, and that you merely studied one side of a two-sided question in freshman biology and accepted what was funneled into your mind without question. And when I do, I'm going to make you EAT those words!"[13]

It is noteworthy that Armstrong earnestly desired to read the Bible and see for himself what it said concerning important issues. But he possessed no formal education and certainly was not trained in interpreting the Bible. That, of course, did not mean that he could not study the Bible, nor did it mean that he could not grasp the truths of Scripture. What it should have precluded, however, was the dogmatism that characterized his conclusions. We say this in retrospect, because we know some seventy years later the direction in which those conclusions led: a private Bible study turned out to be not so private.

Armstrong did decide, after much research and thought, that the

theory of evolution was incorrect and the Bible's account was literally
true. He does admit, however, that the arguments in favor of evolution
were appealing at first.[14] After a more careful study, he "disproved" the
theory.[15]

Interestingly, Armstrong reached the conclusion that evolution was
false one year after the highly publicized Scopes trial in July 1925, in
which John T. Scopes, a Tennessee schoolteacher, was found guilty of
violating the law by teaching evolution in his classroom. Hertha clearly
did not agree with the court's decision in the Scopes trial, but her belief
certainly reflected the popular opinion of the day. Armstrong never
referred to the Scopes trial, but he was no doubt aware of it, as it was
covered in the papers almost daily.

Armstrong also reached his own verdict on the sabbath. Having
studied the topic day and night for six solid months (according to his
later claim), he concluded that the Bible not only plainly taught a
Saturday observance of the sabbath, but such an observance was
absolutely mandated. For Armstrong this became the very mark of
identity for the true believer and the one true church.

Other doctrines he came to embrace included the conviction that the
holy days and festivals of the Old Testament are binding today and that
at death an unbeliever does not suffer eternally but simply dies without
ongoing or lasting punishment. This latter teaching would prove
comforting to many who would feel they were already suffering a
financial hell on earth with the advent of the Great Depression.

Armstrong now turned his attention to the doctrine of baptism. After
studying his Quaker heritage and speaking with Adventist, Quaker and
Baptist ministers, he decided that the best understanding was to be had
by the Baptists. He asked the minister to baptize him in 1927. Armstrong was not consciously becoming a Baptist through this act,
however. He understood that he was being baptized into Christ, not
into the Baptist faith.[16]

Then began his quest for the one true church on earth. Armstrong
reasoned that the true church is to be distinguished by certain marks.
These he found in the Old Testament law, chiefly the Ten Command-
ments. "Remember the Sabbath day and keep it holy" stood out from
all the rest. The observance of a Saturday sabbath would turn out to be

one of the hallmarks of Armstrong's WCG.

In his quest for the true church on earth, Armstrong now had a criterion. All churches that practiced worship on Sundays were immediately excluded from consideration. This of course eliminated most churches throughout Christendom. Armstrong was left with only three religious groups: Seventh-day Adventism, Seventh Day Baptists and the Church of God.

Armstrong concluded that the Seventh-day Adventists followed the teachings of Ellen G. White and not the Bible. The Seventh Day Baptists were ruled out because they really did not differ from other churches of Protestant Christianity in any way save the issue of the sabbath. In the end, for Armstrong, the denomination that was left standing was the Church of God, specifically the Church of God in Stanberry, Missouri. This small sect would lend its name to what would shortly be Armstrong's new movement.

The fact that this church had fewer than two thousand members caused Armstrong no small consternation at first. But Jesus had said, "Strait is the gate, and narrow is the way, which leadeth unto life, and few there be that find it" (Mt 7:14 KJV). Armstrong spent the three years following his baptism in teaching and writing, all the while developing his distinctive theology.

Several family events during these years influenced his thinking, especially what he later referred to as Loma's miraculous healing. In 1927 or thereabouts, Loma became extremely ill with blood poisoning, which she had contracted after pricking her finger with a rose thorn. A doctor grimly told Herbert that she would not live another day.

Not knowing what else to do, Armstrong reluctantly consented to having a visiting couple lay hands on Loma and pray for her. The next morning, Loma got up and went about her daily business as if she had never been ill. Armstrong was so struck by this that he determined thenceforth to rely on God through prayer and never to seek medical attention again.

On October 13, 1928, Loma gave birth to Richard David. The Armstrongs' fourth child and second son, Garner Ted, was born on February 9, 1930. Armstrong wrote that the birth of "Dick" was "the happiest day of my life."[17] That happiness would end in sorrow thirty years later, when Richard was killed in an automobile accident. As for Garner Ted, there would also be triumphs and tragedies. At two and a half he was stricken with pneumonia. According to Armstrong, he prayed for his son, the fever left, and young Garner Ted, who had not yet begun to talk, began to piece together syllables, words and phrases. Thereafter he grew up and developed quite normally.

In 1928 Armstrong had begun writing articles for the Stanberry church's newsletter, *The Bible Advocate.* He claims in his *Autobiography* that he had put the Stanberry church to two tests before deciding to join. The first concerned observance of the Old Testament feast days, which Armstrong claimed was mandated by Scripture. The second was the doctrine of Anglo-Israelism, on which Armstrong submitted a three-hundred-page manuscript. Other members of the Church of God were not as convinced as he was, however. Armstrong quickly grew dissatisfied with the Stanberry leadership.

Armstrong later insisted that the editor of *The Bible Advocate* had acknowledged the periodical's mistakes but would not publish corrections or retractions of these errors. Armstrong claimed that the editor admitted that Armstrong's thesis on Anglo-Israelism was also accurate but took no action to study, consider or adopt the doctrine. It was not long before Armstrong reached the conclusion that even the Church of God was not correct on what he considered weighty and important matters. Yet Armstrong's claims do not match statements of denominational leaders in the Stanberry group:

> Several years ago this man was a minister of our faith. However, he jumped the track on British Israelism and a few other connected subjects. . . .
>
> Mr. Armstrong became convinced through his own personal Bible study, that the feast Days are still to be kept by Christians today. He wanted to preach this doctrine, and this resulted in his ministerial license being revoked by the Oregon Conference Board.[18]

It should be pointed out that Armstrong's exhaustive paper on Anglo-Israelism relied rather heavily on sources external to the Bible. This would be perfectly acceptable, except that he failed to acknowledge this fact. One former member of the WCG recently commented that he had once compared Armstrong's *The United States and Britain in Prophecy* with J. H. Allen's *Judah's Scepter and Joseph's Birthright* (sixteenth edition published in 1917). "The similarities were so remarkable," he stated, "that one can easily conclude that Armstrong practically copied it without ever giving Allen due credit."[19]

A series of evangelistic meetings conducted during the summer of 1933 on a farm owned by Elmer Fisher and his wife outside of Eugene, Oregon, would later be viewed as the birth and beginning of the WCG. The Fishers had invited Armstrong to preach in a one-room building. Armstrong walked about the countryside, inviting people from the area to come to the meetings. By the end of the summer about twenty-five people were attending. These would be the charter members of the new Church of God.

The Church Born on the Air

Armstrong soon had an opportunity to display his charismatic voice on a radio station in Eugene. The station manager was so impressed with Armstrong's radio presence that he charged him the token amount of three dollars to broadcast Sunday-morning worship. This was the start of a radio ministry that would eventually be broadcast worldwide. Echoing a prophetic theme, Armstrong named his radio program *The Radio Church of God.*

Preaching and broadcasting were followed by the aggressive young salesman-turned-minister's desire to be published. *The Bulletin of the Churches of God in Oregon* became the forerunner of the magazine that would be the hallmark of the WCG, *The Plain Truth.* The first mimeographed issue of the latter rolled off a borrowed mimeograph press on February 1, 1934, to a circulation of 106 readers.

That year was important to Armstrong for another reason. He believed that on the first Sunday in January of 1934, the first preaching of the "true" gospel took place since the time of the New Testament, specifically since A.D. 69. He claimed that the church since that time had been "in the wilderness," but God had promised to preserve his little flock and had done so by calling Herbert W. Armstrong to be God's one true prophet for today.

With a growing sense of mission coupled with a slow but positive response to the radio ministry and increased circulation of *The Plain Truth,* Armstrong decided it was time to expand. His original approach on the radio had been to aim at church audiences. With the marketing skills he had learned over the years, he decided to shift the focus of the ministry by targeting both the radio broadcast and the magazine to the unchurched.

In 1935 Armstrong purchased a small schoolhouse, where he continued to preach and the little flock began to grow. The first group of Armstrong's followers were asked to pledge fifty dollars per month. One hard and fast rule he established from the beginning was that funds were not to be solicited from his listening audience. Members, however, would be expected to tithe, and later to triple-tithe, their income. Nevertheless, financial struggles continued in those early years. The publication of *The Plain Truth* was halted in 1935 and remained in hiatus until January 1938. With a monthly ministry budget of only three hundred dollars, Armstrong was forced to put his family to work. He also made desperate appeals to his small band of followers for more support, or else, he made clear, the ministry would have to fold.

Things turned for the better in 1940, when Armstrong acquired a 1,000-watt broadcast on a radio station in Seattle. *The Plain Truth* moved from the mimeograph to the printing press and was now being mailed out to close to three thousand readers. Circulation began to increase monthly. For the next several years Armstrong's lifestyle was frantic: he drove back and forth between Seattle and Eugene each week to meet the demands of his radio broadcasts and preaching ministry. He managed to keep up this routine for several years, but the exhausting schedule took its toll. He started to make the trip by train and soon decided to hasten things even more by flying. His first airplane trip from Seattle to Portland took place on December 7, 1941, that "day of infamy" when Japan bombed Pearl Harbor.

Armstrong's daughter Dorothy became engaged to a University of Oregon law student, Vern Mattson. Vern had enlisted in the marines, and Dorothy wished to travel to California to visit him. Her parents decided to accompany her, but Loma shortly thereafter returned to Eugene, leaving Herbert and daughter behind.

Armstrong recalls meeting his future son-in-law: "When he came to the car, he virtually ignored me. I made some embarrassed comment in an effort to be friendly. 'Look, I'm not marrying *you,* I'm going to marry your daughter!' he snapped."[20] Armstrong dismissed this rudeness because he knew Mattson was under extreme pressure in boot camp. He came to regard Mattson as an unusually friendly person, and Mattson eventually worked for the WCG as controller of Ambassador College and business manager of the radio program.

The California trip was important for another reason, for during this time Armstrong made arrangements to begin broadcasting in Hollywood and decided to change the format of the show. He changed the name from *Radio Church of God* to *The World Tomorrow.* The results of the Hollywood broadcast were remarkable. Armstrong's message of hope for "tomorrow's world" found a receptive audience among many who were experiencing uncertainty and anxiety concerning the future.

Armstrong's empire grew rapidly, despite the fact that other cults were spreading competing claims throughout America. These groups included the rapidly growing Watchtower Bible and Tract Society (Jehovah's Witnesses), the Church of Jesus Christ of Latter-day Saints (Mormons) and numerous other cults and sects that would also would find a home and a following on the soil Armstrong believed was exclusively his own for the preaching of the truth God had revealed to him. Nevertheless, the WCG would witness its greatest growth in the decades following the 1940s.

When Armstrong later returned to Eugene, he learned that responses to the radio ministry were coming in from all over the country. Yet his small staff and still rather limited budget prevented him from meeting all the demands for literature and answers to correspondence.

In 1946, which Armstrong called "the year of beginnings," the radio broadcast began to go out to the entire country, six days a week. At the same time Armstrong embarked on a baptizing tour. At some point on this tour, Armstrong conceived the notion of an institution for higher learning. "I knew God was leading me to start a college that would be His college."[21] His immediate thought was to look for a location in California, where there would be access to Hollywood and larger print shops. The only problem was that as a place to live, neither Los Angeles nor Hollywood was appealing to the Armstrongs. But Pasadena was, and it was right nearby.

Ambassador College

When Armstrong arrived in California after the baptizing tour, a real estate agent showed him a property on Pasadena's Orange Grove Boulevard in a section known as "Millionaire Row." The building had been constructed by a Mr. Fowler, who was president of the International Harvester Corporation. Mrs. Fowler was the daughter of the founder of International Harvester, Cyrus McCormick. The fact that Armstrong managed to negotiate the purchase of this land and building for $100,000 when he had no money is remarkable. In fact, the chapters in Armstrong's autobiography relating to the founding of his three colleges constitute the most interesting reading in both of his thick volumes.

Ambassador College was founded in 1947, not as a Bible college for the exclusive training of ministers but as a liberal arts school. Armstrong believed it is presumptuous to "choose" the ministry, for it is a calling from God. Nevertheless, Ambassador would certainly include a school of theology for those who had such a call.

Before classes actually began on the Pasadena campus, an attempt was made to found a second campus in Switzerland. This mission, which involved an adventuresome trip on the *Queen Elizabeth* with Loma in early 1947, ended in failure. The Armstrongs returned to Pasadena and opened Ambassador College's doors for the first time on October 8, 1947.[22] Because the academic year had started late and most of the enrolled students had moved on, the first class had eight faculty and only four students.

Although the Switzerland venture had failed, Armstrong would succeed in establishing two other campuses also called Ambassador College: one in St. Albans, England (established 1960), and the other in Big Sandy, Texas (established 1964). The peak year for attendance at all three campuses occurred in 1974, with fourteen hundred students.

Both the St. Albans and Big Sandy campuses have been closed, and the Pasadena campus has also been closed and put up for sale. With the reforms of the 1980s and 1990s, efforts were made to keep the

Pasadena campus open, but the measures taken by the Tkach administration proved to be too little, too late. (These measures included
gaining a much-sought-after accreditation in January 1994 that Armstrong had stubbornly refused for years.)

Garner Ted Armstrong

Even a quick recap of the history of the WCG would be incomplete
without a survey of the influence of Armstrong's second son and fourth
child. During his formative years the younger Armstrong wanted
nothing to do with his father's religion; he was caught up in the glitz
and glitter of Hollywood. Marion McNair notes,

> Ted's earliest memories would be of his father as a minister of that
> small church group which later seceded from the Oregon Confer-
> ence.
>
> Ted, . . . smothered with attention from teacher and parents alike,
> developed an inordinately strong sense of self-assurance. In his later
> school years this was transformed into an irrepressible measure of
> cockiness and conceit. True to the tradition of his father, he developed
> a strong outward show of self-sufficiency.[23]

Many children born during the Depression experienced much adver-
sity. In young Ted's life, financial hardship was coupled with the
stigma of his father's identity as a preacher, and an odd one at that.
Most conventional denominations and ministers he knew of did not get
wrapped up with the strange interpretations of the Bible that his father
was becoming known for. Furthermore, most other churches did not
meet in old rented facilities.

During the 1940s, when the ministry was starting to take off, Garner
Ted grew accustomed to the fact that his father and mother were
consumed with the work of ministry and had little time for much else.
Later, Garner Ted said that he had been ashamed of his father's work
and never read a single issue of *The Plain Truth*. He wanted to get
involved in the movie industry. He applied for the position of pageboy
at CBS in Hollywood. But by the time of his senior year of high school,
the fourth child of Herbert and Loma decided to join the navy in order
to get away from his father.[24] However, after three years he left the navy
and returned to Pasadena, disillusioned about life.

In later years, Garner Ted reported that at this point he had decided to reconsider the message his father had been preaching. He claimed that through his own investigation of the Bible, he arrived at the conclusion that his father had been right all along in his interpretations and the unusual doctrines that emerged from them. Some, however, have maintained that a secure job with a promising future gave Garner Ted sufficient motivation for seeing things his father's way.

Garner Ted went to work in the mail room of the WCG in 1952. There he began to put his managerial and communications skills to work and was soon promoted to office manager. In that same year Ted enrolled in Ambassador College and went through the entire curriculum, earning a B.A. (1956), followed by an M.A. and Ph.D., all at Ambassador.

As early as January 1958, the flamboyant and charismatic voice of Garner Ted Armstrong was dominating the airwaves on *The World Tomorrow,* and in that same month he was appointed to be the first vice president directly under his father. Yet despite the impressive title, Herbert had no intention of giving his son, or anyone else for that matter, any real power. He alone would continue to rule and lead the WCG as he saw fit, with little influence from any subordinates, even his own son.

In 1968 Armstrong appointed seven more vice presidents. Garner Ted was renamed executive vice president, but this was again more window dressing than actual power. It was ironic that the supposed second in command was sandwiched between his father and executives with inferior titles who actually possessed more power than he did. In the late 1960s pressure began to mount in the organization, and each day was marked by a thick atmosphere of animosity between father and son and between Garner Ted and the other vice presidents. Then the real trouble began.

Rumors began circulating throughout the WCG that Garner Ted Armstrong had not been faithful to his wife.[25] In July 1971 Herbert felt compelled to confront his son with his infidelity, which had formerly been known only by the top leaders.[26] He gave Garner Ted a two-month leave of absence from his job.

The year 1972 was to mark the end of the "second nineteen-year cycle," in which, according to Herbert's prophecies, the WCG would

be raptured and removed to Petra in the Holy Land. The only disap-
pearance to occur that year, however, was the rapture of Garner Ted
from his job once again.

In early 1972 father and son met in Big Sandy, Texas, where Herbert
relayed an ultimatum to Garner Ted which amounted to either getting
his life back in order within the space of one year or being terminated
altogether from the WCG ministry. The WCG did not disclose the
nature of Garner Ted's problems. He was said simply to be "in the
bonds of Satan."

Garner Ted returned to the organization after only several months.
Apparently he had thought many issues through and sorted them out.
This time he was ready to submit to his father's authority. He was even
given decision-making power, and the only way that decisions on his
part could be revoked was through his father's veto. As Garner Ted
acquired more power, he proceeded to remove many executives from
positions of responsibility.

The Systematic Theology Project
One of Garner Ted's accomplishments in the 1970s was called the
Systematic Theology Project (STP). The resulting document proposed
changes in the WCG and constituted an attempt at constructing just
what its title suggested, a systematic presentation of WCG theology.
Apparently the proposed changes were not known to the elder Armstrong at first.

The table of contents reads like a systematic theology, with such
topics as "Primary Doctrines of God," "Jesus Christ," "The Holy
Spirit," "Man," "Angels," "Salvation," "The Kingdom of God," "The
Law of God," "The Christian" and "The Church of God." The changes
proposed were not significant by today's standards in the WCG; they
still largely reflected Armstrong's theology. When Armstrong learned
of the STP document, however, he labeled it as "Slowly Turning
Protestant." He immediately dismissed it, regarding it as contrary to
his own teachings.

Some WCG ministers were earning Ph.D.s at this time. Armstrong
stopped this practice as well in the early 1980s. The significance of the
STP document is not that it contributed to any changes in the WCG

but that it represented an attempt to make changes. It also demonstrated once again how very much in control of the WCG Herbert Armstrong was, and how little real power Garner Ted had with his father in charge.

Storm Clouds

If Armstrong had known about his son's problem with sexual immorality years before it came to light, why did he allow Garner Ted to rise through the ranks in an organization that was supposed to be God's true church on earth? The answer to that question, or the failure to answer it adequately, became one of many factors that would shortly lead to internal crisis in the WCG.

In the 1970s, news concerning religion and sexual misconduct still had an ability to shock the general public. The Jim Bakker and Jimmy Swaggart scandals had not yet occurred, nor were newspapers yet reporting sexual abuse cases involving Roman Catholic priests and young children. Garner Ted's improprieties were largely eclipsed by the Watergate scandal, the Vietnam War casualties reported almost daily, and the threat of nuclear holocaust. Still, these issues could not keep the members of the WCG from noticing what was happening within their own ranks, as the 1970s proved to be the most volatile decade yet for their church.

The quashing of the STP project was only one example of how strongly Armstrong reacted against changes and liberalizing tendencies in the WCG. Rather intense theological conflicts broke out in 1974 concerning the proper dating of Pentecost and, more significant, rules governing the marriage of divorced members. Armstrong had previously taken a hard-line approach on the latter, maintaining that members who were divorced and remarried must dissolve the relationship with the new spouse because the new marriage was tantamount to being an adulterous affair. In the mid-1970s, however, Armstrong changed this ruling; his personal concern with the issue is discussed below.

A number of ministers resigned at this time, stating that they could no longer tolerate Garner Ted's sexual misconduct and the way money was being squandered, and that they had had fundamental disagreements with certain doctrines.[27] This set in motion a mass resignation of lay members as well. It is estimated that about five thousand members left the WCG in the next several years. Some started new ministries of their own.[28]

As the turbulent decade of the 1970s continued, things changed dramatically in America. The Vietnam conflict ended. Nixon had resigned in disgrace, and in 1976 Jimmy Carter was elected and touted by the media as the "born-again" president. Then came the tragic news of the death of 913 people in Jonestown, Guyana, in 1978, leaving Americans curious, confused and all too painfully aware of the destructive nature of religious cults. The media began to pay more attention to the activities of cults and sects. This would have been a good time for Armstrong and the WCG to behave.

In December 1978 a suit was filed in Los Angeles Superior Court against Herbert Armstrong and his legal counsel, attorney Stanley Rader, Armstrong's personal financial adviser and hand-picked number-two man in the WCG after Garner Ted was removed. The charge was that Armstrong and Rader had both diverted millions of dollars from the church's funds for their personal use. The court placed the WCG in receivership. However, complications in the law forced the attorney general of California to drop the suit. The court ruled in the WCG's favor and against the state for failing to show sufficient cause of action against Rader's firm. Rader was paid $750,000, two-thirds of which went toward paying his back taxes. He immediately resigned his office and stepped down.[29]

Loma Armstrong had died in April 1967. Ten years later to the month, in April 1977, Armstrong, at the age of eighty-nine, announced that he was ready to marry a second time. His new bride was a thirty-nine-year-old divorcée named Ramona Martin.

Armstrong had understandably filled his autobiography with references to and photos of Loma, his first wife, and his children. However, even in the 1986 edition there are no pictures of his second wife. In the work's sole reference to her and to his second marriage, Armstrong writes:

> This almost constant travel (last year 300 out of 365 days) and loneliness has reawakened me to the serious need God recognized when He said, "It is not good that a man should not be alone."

Directly or indirectly, you brethren are all my sons and daughters in the Lord. But I am nonetheless human. . . . People do sometimes forget an apostle has personal needs.

Of course no one could take the place of my beloved wife of fifty years. But the work of God must go on, finishing the great commission God has committed to me. . . . And now God has graciously provided the wife to be constantly at my side—a woman truly led by God's Holy Spirit. We have given the matter much time, to be sure it has grown into true love and like-minded rapport, as well as definitely sure it is God's will.

This is to announce my marriage to Ramona Martin, in an informal and simple ceremony, attended by only our respective families on Sunday, April 17. [entry dated May 16, 1977][30]

Armstrong married Ramona one year after the WCG ended its ban on remarriage by those who had been divorced. As noted above, before 1974 the WCG had issued a very clearly worded policy that new members who were divorced and remarried were to dissolve their current marriages and make attempts, where possible, to remarry their original spouses. Hundreds of families were broken up due to this ruling. The revised 1976 policy read, in part: "The church accepts new converts in whatever marital state they enter the church. . . . A previously divorced person who has entered fellowship is free to remarry within the church."[31] Armstrong had been dating Ramona previous to the time of the new ruling by the WCG, actually several years before the ruling. Interestingly, Garner Ted officiated at the wedding in Tucson, Arizona.

Within five years, however, "true love and like-minded rapport" had soured. Armstrong filed for divorce, citing as reasons Ramona's unbelief and unwillingness to submit to her husband's leadership. The facts of the divorce proceedings were well published in newspapers at the time. But there is possibly another explanation as to why their marriage disintegrated so rapidly.

A book by David Robinson, *Herbert Armstrong's Tangled Web,* accused Armstrong of incest with his daughter Dorothy during the 1930s, when she was a teenager. The WCG leaders unsuccessfully attempted to have Robinson's book blocked in court.

Robinson was not the only one to publish disclosures about Armstrong. Attorney Jack Kessler, a former member, then disfellowshipped, also alleged that Armstrong had committed incest with Dorothy. In a letter to the board of directors of the WCG, dated December 30, 1981, Kessler wrote of Armstrong's "incestuous intercourse with his daughter during the first ten years of his ministry."[32] Former staff member Marion McNair and a layman, John Tuit, also accused Armstrong of gross sexual improprieties.[33]

Those who wish to learn more about this issue should consult Robinson's book; we must reiterate that Robinson's and Kessler's allegations concerning Armstrong's incest are, legally speaking, *only* allegations. When we interviewed some prominent members of the WCG, they shrugged their shoulders when this subject was brought up, saying, "It's never been proven," or "It was Dorothy's word against her father's." What is certain, however, is this. No member of the WCG ever came forward to deny the charges during the time of the court action, at least not with any hard evidence.

Garner Ted was also aware of the news. Over dinner in 1971, his sister related to him all the details of what had happened between her and her father when she was a teenager. Garner Ted remained silent concerning his sister's confession for seven years.

Things came to a head in 1978, when Garner Ted became embroiled in an extremely heated argument with his father. The elder Armstrong threatened to destroy his son by going public with news about Garner Ted's sexual escapades. Garner Ted could harbor his secret no longer. In graphic language he began shouting out what his father had done to his sister.

Herbert, apparently stunned by the fact that Garner Ted held this trump card and knew so much, managed to mutter that there were times when he had grown apart from God. After this, according to Garner Ted, the hatred resulting from this encounter separated father and son for good. Herbert would live the last eight years of his life without seeing his son again.

Garner Ted retreated to Tyler, Texas, where he founded the Church of God International (COGI). He gained an immediate if not significant following. Membership never amounted to more than three thousand in one hundred congregations. In Canada there are about six hundred members spread over eight congregations, and there are only two hundred members in six congregations in other countries. Never again would Garner Ted return to the WCG. He has dropped out of the WCG picture so completely that even present leaders said that they knew next to nothing and were unaware of some of the most basic facts about Garner Ted's current status.

Filing for divorce is relatively easy. Obtaining one, in this case, proved to be considerably more difficult. Stanley Rader and Ramona allegedly conspired in 1981 to have Herbert Armstrong declared mentally incompetent and removed from office. The divorce petition was filed largely in retaliation for this.

The details of the divorce were sordid. Armstrong charged Ramona with attempting to steal property from him. A trial ensued; Armstrong was ordered to appear, though his attorney, Allen Browne, pleaded that his client was physically unable to stand trial because the stress might cause the ninety-one-year-old pastor general a fatal heart attack. Aware that Armstrong was still traveling rather extensively given his age, the judge ordered him to appear at a deposition in Tucson, where Ramona was living. The case focused largely on details of a settlement concerning the Tucson home, purchased in 1977, the year they were married. After two years and millions of dollars in legal fees, Armstrong was granted his much-sought-after divorce.

Resurgence

The more amazing story in all of this melodrama is the fact that the Armstrong empire did not suffer severely, as one would expect given that the news media were busy publishing the details of Armstrong's sexual and financial woes.[34] In fact, successful marketing strategies enabled the WCG membership to soar to over seventy thousand.

There is some discrepancy in figures concerning the circulation of *The Plain Truth*. Some claim that 8.2 million copies were circulated at one point. We called the WCG administration to ask. They said that the highest circulation rose to slightly over six million.

Why did the WCG experience a resurgence despite the problems it had been experiencing? Because Herbert Armstrong was God's anointed in the eyes of many of his devotees. He was an aging leader who was energetic and and still very much in charge. Despite pressure from the media, attacks from within and without, Herbert continued to weather the storms of controversy. He preached, wrote and traveled into his nineties, right up till the time of his death.

Add to this the loyalty of his staff. Armstrong's closest colaborers at the Pasadena headquarters continued to work hard to promulgate the doctrines of the church. They succeeded in addressing immediate needs of the rank-and-file members who were not particularly attuned to or interested in the problems of Armstrong's personal life. Most members scattered throughout the United States and the world were concerned that the church continue to support their pastors and that these pastors continue to meet their spiritual needs on a daily basis. Loyalty to their aging leader was not going to be easily shattered.

THREE

Anatomy of
a Cult

*The strictest right
is the greatest wrong.*
MARTIN LUTHER

*I*t is often said that the WCG was formerly a "cult." The church has
since claimed that it has moved on to becoming a denomination within
the fold of Protestant Christendom. Just what is a cult anyway? This
is a hotly debated issue. Alan Gomes, in his *Unmasking the Cults*,
provides the working definition we accept:

> A cult of Christianity is a group of people, which claiming to be
> Christian, embraces a particular doctrinal system taught by an
> individual leader, group of leaders, or organization, which (system)
> denies (either explicitly or implicitly) one or more of the central
> doctrines of the Christian faith as taught in the sixty-six books of
> the Bible.[1]

The reason Gomes makes a distinction between a "cult of Christianity"
and other kinds of cults is that there are many cults that have arisen out
of non-Christian religions. Gomes goes on to note cults of Islam, such
as Sufism and the Nation of Islam, and cults of Hinduism, which

include Hare Krishna, Self-Realization Fellowship and the Vedanta Society.[2] Mormonism, Jehovah's Witnesses and the Branch Davidians are examples of cults of Christianity because their teachings began as deviations from teachings of various denominations of Christendom.

Was the WCG a cult of Christianity during the tenure of Herbert W. Armstrong? If we accept Gomes's definition, there is little doubt that the WCG under Armstrong embraced a particular doctrinal system that denied the central doctrines of the Christian faith. If this were not true, the WCG would not have changed its doctrines as it has since Armstrong's time. What follows is a review of Armstrong's teachings and how we distinguish them from traditional Christian beliefs.[3]

In this survey of Armstrong's doctrines we rely on the great creeds of Christendom, using the same method adopted in our *Dictionary of Cults, Sects, Religions and the Occult.* The ecumenical creeds of Christianity have always been used in the Christian church in order to encapsulate the teachings of Jesus and his apostles. The major creeds include the Apostles', Nicene, Athanasian and Chalcedonian. When a group calls itself Christian but cannot accept the doctrines contained in these ancient confessions of the Christian faith, it falls outside the boundaries of what is to be considered orthodox in Christ's church. Armstrong himself was so convinced that the creeds were products of a pagan form of Constantinian Christianity that he never stopped to consider their gracious words and the beautiful way they articulate the fundamental articles of the Christian faith.

The creeds were confessed by the early Christians for at least three basic reasons. First, throughout the early church, the Bible was not in codex (book) form, and very few people possessed copies of Scripture texts. The creeds (the apostles' doctrine, as referred to in Acts 2:41-42) were taught so that Christians could recite and confess the articles of the faith that they had come to know. Second, the creeds enabled the believers to undergo what was known in the early church as "catechesis" or instruction in Christian doctrine (see 2 Tim 3:16). Third, the creeds functioned apologetically—that is, they were used to defend the faith when fundamental truths of Christianity were challenged by pagans and heretics. It is ironic that Armstrong himself attacked and condemned much of the paganism that the creeds themselves oppose.

Of course, we cite Scripture often throughout this book, not only the creeds. But use of the ecumenical creeds has enabled us to avoid the pitfalls of Bible proof-texting. Citing Scripture, a method almost always used in Christian apologetics, is generally necessary but occasionally unhelpful. When Scripture is quoted to counter the claims of the cultist, the passage is almost invariably viewed through the lens of the particular denomination or religious tradition of the critic. The combination of creeds and Scripture, from which the creeds were formulated, provide a broader base for delineating what Christians believe, confess and teach over against what the various cults of Christianity and non-Christian religions teach. We do not say this to downplay the role of the Bible, especially since we are Lutherans. It was Luther who championed the doctrine of *sola Scriptura* (the Bible alone). By the use of the creeds, however, we can draw on the orthodox church's earliest expressions of its understanding of Scripture.

The Doctrine of God

For Armstrong, God is a family. Christians believe that God is three Persons—Father, Son and Holy Spirit. Christians since the second century have called this the doctrine of the Trinity. However, Armstrong argued that the word *trinity* is not in the Bible. He contended that the belief in God as triune was borrowed from pagan mystery religions and foisted upon the Christian church at the Council of Nicaea in A.D. 325.[4]

Furthermore, Armstrong said, the idea that God is a family of three Persons is false because it limits God. Citing a Hebrew name for God, *Elohim,* Armstrong argued that it meant "family, church, or group."[5] This group is not just three, but many. It is now comprised of *two* Persons, the Father and the Son. Ultimately, however, God's family will be everyone who is born again (see below). God then, becomes "many thousands" of persons who will one day be God as he reproduces himself in and through his family. At the time of the end, Christ will return, abolishes the government of Lucifer and restore the kingdom, and all the begotten sons of God will then be born again of God, with God's kingdom and government ruling forever.

Armstrong viewed the Trinity as an outright enemy of the Gospel:

"The Trinity doctrine . . . destroys the very gospel of Jesus Christ! His gospel is the good news of the now soon-coming Kingdom of God— the only hope for this world and its mixed up mankind!"[6]

Armstrong's denial of the Trinity immediately alienated the WCG from traditional Christianity. First, it implied that there is really no distinction between God and creation, at least the creation of human beings. In Romans 1:25 Paul distinguishes between the Creator and creation and says that the great sin of humankind is the very failure to make this distinction. When Christians die, they do not become God. They are united with God in order to worship and enjoy God in his fullness and glory. One who worships is qualitatively different from the One being worshiped. If this were not so, the very concept of worship would be meaningless.

Armstrong's argument that the word *trinity* is not found in the Bible and therefore is not biblical is common to most cults and sects that deny the Trinity. It is certainly true that the word *trinity* does not appear in the Bible. But that does not mean the *concept* does not. There are many places in the Bible that allude to the idea of God as a triune being—for example, Matthew 3:16-17 and 28:19, John 15:26, 2 Corinthians 13:14 and Galatians 4:6.

If the Trinity is not a true biblical teaching, then clearly Jesus Christ is not God in the flesh. But Jesus is recognized as God throughout the Bible (Is 7:4; 9:6; Mic 5:2; Jn 1:1; 5:18, 21-24; 8:58; 10:30; 17:5; Phil 2:11; Col 2:9; 1 Tim 3:16; Heb 1:3; etc.). Therefore the beliefs confessed at the early church councils was not, as Armstrong believed, doctrines that were pagan or innovative. The church fathers merely *recognized what was already written in the Bible when they met in council over this issue.* It is true that the church fathers used technical language and introduced the controversial word *ousia* (substance) to assist the church in understanding the very difficult concept of God as one essence and yet manifested in three Persons *(hypostasis).* This understanding is clearly stated in the Athanasian Creed: "The catholic faith is this, that we worship one God in three persons and three persons in one God."

Often issues are addressed in the church when error arises. The Trinity debate was addressed when false teachers denied the Trinity.

Among the first of these was Arius (c. 250-c. 336), who had been ordained a deacon in the church of Alexandria and taught that Jesus could not be God because he was not eternal, as God is. Arius believed there was a time when Jesus did not exist. Arius was challenged by St. Athanasius (c. 296-373), who was the bishop of Alexandria. The Council of Nicaea considered the arguments of both Arius and Athanasius and recognized that Arius's views were in error. The Nicaean Council condemned Arianism in A.D. 325.

Armstrong has sometimes been accused of repeating the errors of Arius. If this were the case, the WCG would be teaching the same thing the Jehovah's Witnesses teach, which we just summarized above—that there was a time when Jesus did not exist. Armstrong, however, did not teach this, and the reason is interesting. Gomes points out in his crisp analysis of Armstrong's doctrine of the Trinity that even though it sounds much like that of the Jehovah's Witnesses, an important distinction must be made between the two groups:

Armstrong's *positive* teaching has little in common with the Watchtower.

Armstrong seems to start out on a much more orthodox footing, ascribing both deity and eternality to Christ. Speaking of Christ as the Word in John 1:1, Armstrong states: "The Greek word [in John 1:1] is 'Logos' . . . who co-existed with the Father from eternity—who always existed—who is one with the Father . . . the 'WORD,' who was the ETERNAL . . . the very GOD himself—HE WAS MADE FLESH" In direct contradiction to the Watchtower position, Armstrong even applies the title "Yahweh" to Jesus.[7]

Here we have a most unusual combination. Armstrong denied the doctrine of the Trinity and apparently believed that Jesus was eternal. Most cults of Christianity deny the Trinity precisely in order to deny the deity of Christ. Ultimately, Armstrong did not distinguish Jesus' divinity from that of believers, who too will take up their place as gods in the one eternal family.

Jesus Christ

Armstrong and the WCG taught that Jesus was born of a virgin. After Jesus' crucifixion and death, however, the body that had been taken from the cross and sealed in a tomb was not the body that was raised from the dead. "It was *Christ Himself* who was *dead*. He was *revived*. Nowhere does the Scripture say He was alive and active, or that God had Him get back into the human *body*, that died and was now resurrected. . . . Jesus Christ was *dead*—but *revived!* "[8] The body that was raised from the dead, according to Armstrong, was a different body. After Jesus' resurrection, he possessed a single divine nature.

According to the clear teachings of Scripture, this was a grave error on Armstrong's part. We could not possibly quote all the Bible passages—and all the church fathers who quote from those passages—that demonstrate that the resurrected body of Jesus was indeed the body that had been crucified on the cross. Consider just a couple of texts: In John 2:19-21, Jesus makes it plain that God will raise up his "body" at the resurrection. After the resurrection, doubting Thomas could not continue to doubt when he saw Jesus' pierced hands and feet (Jn 20:27).

How the divine and human natures of Christ are related to each other is complex but an extremely important issue in Christianity. For the purposes of this book it is crucial that we cover it briefly so that we might understand Armstrong's errors.

In the second through fourth centuries, different ideas arose concerning how Jesus' humanity and divinity were to be understood. There were those who believed that Jesus was more divine than he was human. The Christian Gnostics, for example, believed that they possessed a secret knowledge *(gnosis)* that other Christians did not have. The fundamental principle of this secret knowledge was that matter and spirit are radically different from and opposed to each other. For the Gnostics, matter was evil and spirit was good. For Jesus to possess a human nature, then, would be unthinkable, because God could not possibly inhabit such an evil substance as human flesh. Christian Gnostics had little problem in believing that Jesus was divine, but they rejected outright the idea that Christ's divinity was incarnate (enfleshed) in a human body. In other words, the Gnostics emphasized Christ's divinity at the expense of his humanity.

Other groups in the early church tended toward the other extreme of emphasizing Jesus' humanity at the expense of his divinity. An example of this was the heresy known as modalism or Sabellianism, which held that God existed in three different modes at three different times. He was Father at the time of creation. He took on a new mode of existence by becoming human at the time Jesus was born, and it was Jesus, the human God, who then suffered death on the cross.[9] God became the Holy Spirit, the third mode of existence, after Jesus ascended into heaven.

The Council of Chalcedon, which was held in A.D. 451, was an extremely important council. Here the doctrine of the two natures of Christ was clearly articulated for the Christian church. According to the Council of Chalcedon, the Bible teaches that Christ's divine and human natures are related in such a way that each shares the properties of the other.[10] The human nature participates fully in the divine nature, and the divine nature participates in the human nature. Put another way, the human nature of Christ is truly the nature of the Son of God (divine), and the divine nature is truly the nature of the Son of Man (human). Theologians have called this the *communicatio idiomaticum* (communication of natures), or the personal union of the two natures.

Why does this issue need to be discussed in a book about the WCG? Because Armstrong held that Jesus possessed a single divine nature. Yet at the same time he considered Jesus' shed blood important for the forgiveness of sins:

In order that man might be reconciled to God, Jesus also came for the express purpose of DEATH, by His shed blood paying for us, in our stead, the death penalty we have incurred as the penalty of sin. In order that we might be given God's gift of ETERNAL LIFE, Jesus' resurrection from the dead was necessary before we could receive eternal life.[11]

Correct doctrine is especially important when it relates to the central focus of Christianity—Jesus Christ. When the Bible states, "The blood of Jesus, his Son, purifies us from all sin" (1 Jn 1:7)—which Armstrong apparently believed—a question immediately arises. How can blood, a physical quality of the human person of Jesus, participate at all in salvation if Jesus possesses only a single divine nature? In other words, if the divine nature of Jesus is not connected or related in some way to a human nature, how can human qualities (in this case blood) do something divine such as cleanse from sin?

The importance of the Council of Chalcedon was that it recognized the full implications of what it meant for the divine and human natures of Jesus to each share fully the properties of the other in a "personal union."

The Holy Spirit

Armstrong taught that the Holy Spirit was not a third Person in the Godhead, because God presently consists of two Persons. The Holy Spirit cannot be a Person at all, in fact, because "it" is "poured out." Quoting Acts 2:18, Armstrong asks, "Can you pour out a person from one into another—as from God into those assembled there?"[12]

Armstrong also believed that if the Holy Spirit were a third Person, in addition to limiting God to only three, it would diminish an important role that Jesus plays in the lives of believers. "This *denies* that Christ, through His Holy Spirit actually comes now *into* the converted Christian and does His saving work on the *inside*—'Christ in you the hope of glory' (Colossians 1:27)."[13]

Armstrong's misunderstanding about the nature of the Trinity led to his confusion about the role of the Holy Spirit. For Christendom, the Holy Spirit is indeed a Person as attested to in Scripture (Jn 14:16-18; 16:7-14; Acts 5:3-4). The Spirit gives life to the church and is in fact that Person of the Godhead from whom the church is created (Ephesians 1:13).

The Nicene Creed states wonderfully both who the Holy Spirit is and what the Holy Spirit does. The Holy Spirit is "the Lord and giver of life, who proceeds from the Father and the Son, who with the Father and the Son is worshiped and glorified." Concerning the work of the Spirit, Jesus was "conceived by the Holy Spirit," as he was "born of the Virgin Mary." It is the Holy Spirit who grants to each Christian the very ability to believe (1 Cor 2:10-16). That is why the Nicene Creed connects the Holy Spirit to the "one holy catholic and apostolic church," to "one baptism for the forgiveness of sins" and to "the resurrection from the dead." In other words, the church is the corporate "communion of saints" which receives its very life from the Holy Spirit.

Immortality

The category of immortality involves several important issues. What is humankind? Why did God create human beings? Concerning what humankind essentially is, Armstrong asserted: "Man was made to have a special relationship with his Maker! He was made in the form and shape of God. He was given a spirit to make that relationship possible. . . . But God made MAN of MATTER."[14] Armstrong believed that persons possess souls but denied that the soul is immortal. He taught that at the time a person dies, every part of them dies, including the soul. "Man, formed from material dust of the ground, upon breathing air, BECAME a living soul. It does not say that man is, or has, an *immortal* soul. What was formed from material ground BECAME a soul. . . . Therefore the soul is physical, composed of matter, and can die."[15] Human nature, then, is no different from that of animals in Armstrong's view. Armstrong believed that the concept of an immortal soul was rooted in the pagan philosophy of Plato. At the time of the resurrection, the soul is brought back to live forever. It is only the righteous, however, who are granted the privilege of everlasting life. The wicked die (are annihilated) and remain dead forever.[16]

Armstrong apparently rethought the implications of this issue. Clearly uncomfortable with the teaching that the nature of human beings is no different from that of animals, he shifted a bit and taught that human beings possess a "spirit." This spirit "imparts the power of intellect to the human brain."[17] Spirit affords human beings the capacities for love, morality, God-consciousness, creativity and so on. But why, ultimately, did God create human beings? Armstrong answers definitively: "The purpose of life is that in us God is really recreating *His own kind—reproducing Himself* after *His* own kind—for we are, upon real conversion, actually *begotten* as sons (yet unborn) of God."[18]

Armstrong was in error with respect to his understanding of immortality. Most Christian thinkers have understood the soul to be the spiritual substance, or that part of a human being where God's image (Gen 1:26) resides. Soul and spirit together make up all of what it means to be human. At death, the soul and the body are separated from each other (Eccles 12:7; Lk 23:43; Jn 3:36; Eph 1:3-6; Phil 1:23; 1 Jn 3:2; Rev 14:13). This separation, however, is not permanent. At the time of the resurrection, the soul and the body are joined together once again (Ps 16:11; Mt 25:34; Rom 8:18; 1 Cor 15:51-52; 1 Jn 3:2).

Armstrong did not distinguish between the pagan philosopher Plato's teachings concerning the immortality of the soul and that of St. Paul. The former believed in the *preexistence* of the soul before birth into a human body. Paul, on the other hand, taught that the soul is immortal from the time of birth, when it is formed, and lives on after death (1 Cor 15:42-44, 51-52; Phil 3:21). Other passages teach this as well (Job 19:26-27; Jn 5:29).

Born Again

One of the earliest and most startling teachings of Armstrong was his doctrine of the "new birth." In John 3:3-8 Jesus tells Nicodemus that "no one can see the kingdom of God unless he is born again." This passage has been interpreted in different ways in Christian denominations. Some understand it as a reference to baptism. Others understand it more experientially, referring to a point at which a person professes faith in Christ and is saved. Armstrong's interpretation is unique. He does identify the new birth as baptismal, picking up on the language of John 3:4-6. But where he parts company with any traditional interpretations is his understanding of the new birth as a *future* event not obtainable in this life. "That tremendous, glorious event of being BORN of God is to take place AT THE RESURRECTION OF THE JUST—at the time of Christ's second coming to earth."[19] Armstrong did not deviate from this position throughout the years. Jesus Christ, by his death, was the firstborn member of the family of God, which presently comprises two members, the Father and the Son. Being born again is the way believers will one day also be included in the divine family of God and become gods themselves. In this life a person who comes to faith is, for Armstrong, a "spiritual embryo" who has been "begotten" by God but not yet born again.

Armstrong's interpretation conflicts with the teachings of the Bible and the church. Salvation takes place immediately upon faith in Christ's finished work of redemption. When a Christian is born again, he or she receives something from God: God's righteousness or justifying grace. Paul uses the word *impute,* which means "lay upon, reckon or place upon," to explain this. He describes how God removes sin and places (imputes) righteousness upon the believer (Rom 4:8, 11, 22-24; 5:13). We are not aware of anyone in all of Christendom who understood the imputation of Christ's righteousness to be future rather than present. When Paul writes in Ephesians 2:8-9, "By grace you are saved through faith," the present tense of the verb means that salvation is a present status "imputed" to the believer as soon as grace is conferred, not after he or she dies. The writer to the Hebrews devotes his whole epistle to the teaching that Christ is the great high priest who brings atonement presently to the church through the shedding of his blood.

Hell

Armstrong's confusion with respect to immortality was largely a result of his confusion about the doctrine of hell. In his book *Is There a Real Hellfire?* he rightly points out that the word for hell is the Greek word *Hades* in the New Testament and the word *Sheol* in the Old Testament. He taught that these words really meant grave or burial place, not a place of torment and punishment. For Armstrong, the real hell in the Bible is the one referred to by *Gehenna,* the name of a garbage dump outside Jerusalem, in the Valley of Hinnom, where dead bodies were dumped and burned. While the church teaches that souls who have rejected God will suffer eternally, Armstrong said that Gehenna or the "lake of fire" in Revelation 21:8 is not where the damned will live; rather, it is the place where they will finally die forever.[20]

The Christian faith has historically taught that hell is a place of real eternal torment for the damned.[21] While believers have eternal life, the unbeliever will also live eternally, but in a state of everlasting condemnation (Is 66:24; Mk 9:48; Lk 16:23-24; Jn 3:18; Rev 14:11; 20:10).

Armstrong's basic error was already partially discussed above (see "Immortality"). Also, he failed to distinguish physical death from eternal death, or what the Bible calls the second death: everlasting punishment and torment.

Eternal life and eternal damnation are juxtaposed in the New Testament (Mt 25:46; Jn 3:36). The Apostles' and Nicene creeds both confess the resurrection and eternal life. The Athanasian Creed, however, goes a step further and recognizes the above-cited Scriptures by distinguishing between the two states of eternal life: "Whoever will be saved shall, above all else, hold the catholic faith. Which faith, except everyone keeps whole and undefiled, without doubt he will perish eternally.... And they that have done good will go into life everlasting; and they that have done evil into everlasting fire. This is the catholic faith which, except a man believe faithfully and firmly, he cannot be saved."

Some Protestants have raised a question concerning these last words of the Athanasian Creed by protesting that good works do not save, nor do bad deeds damn. It is faith in Christ's good works that saves us from our bad ones. The Athanasian Creed does not contradict with this but in fact upholds it. The context is key. The good work of which the creed speaks is faith in what is the whole subject of the creed—the confession of God as Father, Son and Holy Spirit. The chief evil deed is simply to deny God as Father, Son and Holy Spirit. This was certainly the error of the unbelieving Jews when they rejected Jesus as the incarnate Son of God (Jn 5:23). It is also the principal error of cults of Christianity that expressly deny the Trinity, as Armstrong did in many of his writings and teachings.[22]

Salvation and the Law

As we have observed, salvation for Armstrong is not a present reality but future. One's life before death is lived in preparation for the future new birth. How does one prepare? Although one is to live in faith, the life Armstrong envisioned is really a life of obedience to the laws of God. Such laws include a strict observance of the Saturday sabbath. Sunday worship, observed in traditional Christendom, was regarded as false worship. Armstrong also taught obedience to the Jewish dietary laws of the Levitical code and observance of the festival days as required for one's salvation. Furthermore, water baptism by immersion was said to be necessary.

Members were expected and required to triple-tithe—to give 30 percent of their income to the church. The WCG taught tithing within a seven-year cycle. The first tithe each year went to headquarters. The second tithe was kept to finance the members' attendance at the holy days.

The third tithe, in the third and sixth year of the seven-year cycle, went to headquarters to support the needy in the church.

A whole host of other requirements were included in the list of things commanded and forbidden for the purpose of procuring salvation in the future. These included laws regarding makeup for women, dress codes, guidelines regarding acceptable music, dating rules and rules against observing certain holidays such as birthdays, Christmas and Easter.

Missing from Armstrong's understanding, but present in the doctrine of salvation as taught, proclaimed and confessed in traditional Christianity, is Jesus Christ as a loving and gracious Savior who died on the cross freely to offer forgiveness of sins to all who believe and call on his name (Jn 1:12-13; 3:16; Rom 3:21-26; Gal 1; 2:21; Eph 2:8-9). Nowhere in the Apostles' or Nicene creeds is there any mentioned about what believers must do for salvation. Instead, the entire corpus of the creeds speaks about what *God has done* and *is doing* in the divine economy of the holy Trinity. The First Article tells us that God the Father is the Creator of all that is; the Second Article tells us that Jesus Christ, in both his person and his work, completed all that was necessary for salvation; the Third Article tells us about the work of the Holy Spirit. All three of these constitute what salvation is for Christianity.

The Sabbath

Under special consideration regarding salvation and the law is the issue of the Saturday sabbath. As we saw in chapter two, this doctrine was a major challenge laid before Armstrong by his first wife, Loma. At the beginning of his "call by God," Armstrong became convinced that virtually all the Protestant churches, and certainly the entire Roman Catholic Church, were false forms of Christianity for many reasons. One of the most important was the failure to practice worship on the sabbath day. His writings on this subject were extensive and varied, and he remained firmly convinced of this doctrine throughout his life. His last words on the subject remained essentially the same as those in his early years. In his "last will and testament," Armstrong writes:

In about A.D. 365 the Catholic Council of Laodicea wrote in one of its most famous canons: "Christians must not judaize by resting on the Sabbath, but must work on that day, rather, honoring the Lord's Day. But if any shall be found to be judaizers, let them be anathema from Christ." This was a virtual sentence to torture and/or death. The false church did not herself put true believers to death, but caused them to be put to death (Rev. 13:15). The decree of A.D. 365 definitely shows that there were true Christians observing the Sabbath.[23]

Contrary to what Armstrong taught, the Saturday sabbath was ordained in the Old Testament for a twofold purpose. Israel was commanded to observe it as a day for worship and for rest (Ex 20:10; 31:13-17; Num 28:9; Lev 23:2; Deut 5:14). One of the hallmarks of Judaism was strict observance of the sabbath. By the time of Jesus in the first century, this observance had gained enormous significance. Jesus even offended the Pharisees by commenting that "the Sabbath was made for man, not man for the Sabbath" (Mk 2:27).

The Jewish leaders were outraged by Jesus' teachings concerning the two pillars of Judaism, the Torah and the temple. Jesus superseded both of these in his own person. Of the temple he said, "Destroy this temple, and I will raise it again in three days" (Jn 2:19). Concerning the law, Jesus repeatedly said, "You have heard that it was said . . . but I say unto you . . ." (see Mt 5). Clearly Jesus' own authority took precedence over the temple, whose veil was rent at the time of the crucifixion, showing that he himself was the new and only access to the Father, and over the law of Moses and the rabbinic interpretations of those laws. Jesus was therefore testifying to and proclaiming his divinity when he said that "the Son of man is Lord even of the Sabbath" (Mk 2:28).

The basic thrust of early Gentile Christianity was a gradual movement away from Jewish rites and rituals, including sabbath observance. The change to worshiping on Sunday, or the "first day of the week," was, like the Old Testament sabbath, done for two reasons. In the early church, Christians gathered on the first day of the week to commemorate the day of the resurrection (the new creation, hence the new sabbath rest) and because the Holy Spirit was given on the Day of Pentecost (Acts 2), on the first day of the week. Paul makes it clear that Christians are free from strict observance of the Old Testament sabbath (Col 2:16). Hebrews 4:1-10 says that Christ himself is the sabbath rest for his church.

The final and most important point regarding Armstrong's interpretation of sabbath was that to insist on the Saturday sabbath is to undermine the finished work of Christ entirely. "I do not set aside the grace of God, for if righteousness could be gained through the law, Christ died for nothing!" (Gal 2:21). To substitute any laws in place of Christ, in hopes of merit or favor in the eyes of God, is what the late Walter Martin called "the new Galatianism." What he meant by this was that in Galatians, Paul strongly condemns false teachers who were trying to subvert the gospel by adding law to grace.[24]

Anglo-Israelism

Anglo-Israelism is the teaching that Anglo-Saxons are the direct descendants of the lost ten tribes of Israel. Armstrong was not the originator of this doctrine, for it has been held by other religious groups and individuals. The idea originated in England in the latter part of the eighteenth century and from there came to America. But Armstrong adopted it wholeheartedly and used it to support the teaching that the WCG itself was foreseen in prophecy as the true church of God today, with Armstrong at the helm as its one true prophet.

Through a series of Bible passages and rather amazing semantic exercises, Armstrong argued in his booklet *The United States and Britain in Prophecy* that Great Britain and the United States are the nations chosen as the lands to which the tribes of Ephraim and Manasseh migrated. When the Assyrians invaded the northern kingdom of Israel in 721 B.C., ten tribes were removed from their homeland and scattered. Quoting Jeremiah 3:11-12 and 31:10, Isaiah 49:3, 6, 12, Psalm 89:25 and other passages, Armstrong argued that the lost tribes migrated to Great Britain, which as a nation seemed to fulfill various prophecies perfectly. The Bible speaks of a seafaring people on the "isles afar off" (Jer 31:10 KJV). Furthermore, since God had established a covenant with Israel, and since the Hebrew word for covenant is *berith,* then the Hebrew word for man, *iysh,* goes logically with *berith* to get *Berith-iysh,* or

British. Saxons is another word whose origins, according to Armstrong, could be traced to prove scriptural references to England. As we said in our previous book:

> Since it was Isaac's seed that God had promised to bless (Gen. 21:12), and if the *i* is dropped, we are left with "saac," and it was "Saac's sons" or Saxons" with whom God had established his covenant. Furthermore, Armstrong insisted that the English throne is the modern day extension of the throne of David, contending that the Stone of Scone, on which Queen Elizabeth II was crowned, was the very stone that Jacob used for a pillow. Later it was transported by the prophet Jeremiah to the British Isles.[25]

Important in Armstrong's understanding of Anglo-Israelism was the fact that after the kingdom was divided into Israel (north) and Judah (south), Israel became two nations. The kingdom of Judah was restored to the southern region after the Babylonian exile, and therefore the Jews of Jerusalem still reside in Palestine. But the northern kingdom was made up of the lost tribes, which migrated to the British Isles. The chief tribe in this migration was Ephraim. Armstrong believed the British Commonwealth had prospered around the world and became powerful in the nineteenth century because this was indeed God's covenant people.[26] He explained that the tribe of Manasseh migrated to the United States when Great Britain began to colonize the New World. Armstrong believed he was linked to the prophetic past and believed God had chosen America, and him personally, to lead the world.

Anglo-Israelism is not hard to refute. Armstrong quoted Greek and Hebrew liberally throughout his writings; because he did not substantiate his remarks about these languages with references to scholarly sources, one gets the impression that he is his own source of authority. Yet Armstrong did not know Greek or Hebrew. Any average student of either of these languages would not dream of making the errors Armstrong made in concluding that the English etymology of *Britain* and *Saxons* led back to biblical languages. An outstanding critique of Anglo-Israelism has been produced by Hebrew scholar David Baron.[27] Yet Armstrong held to this belief with no variation right up to the time of his death.[28]

The Church

Armstrong's doctrine of Anglo-Israelism in part informed his thinking about the church. "And I was led through the years from conversion to understanding God's revelation of these seven biblical mysteries that have baffled the minds of humanity and to find that one and only true Church of God was founded by Jesus Christ on the Day of Pentecost, A.D. 31."[29] Armstrong, like many other cult leaders, held to this belief because he claimed God had called him to be his true prophet for today. All other churches, especially the Roman Catholic Church, are false churches weighed down with doctrinal errors caused by the corruptions of pagan influences on early Christianity.

For Armstrong, false doctrine began to proliferate as early as the first century. He contended that Simon Magus (Acts 8) was immersed in the Babylonian mystery religions and tried to impose these false teachings on the one true church of God in the New Testament. The apostle Peter used discernment in foiling Simon's ambitious plot to purchase a church office, but soon many false teachers began to enter in and corrupt the church.

Armstrong taught that the message of the seven churches in Revelation 1—2 should be understood in a twofold sense. The seven churches located in Asia Minor (present-day Turkey) included Ephesus, Smyrna, Pergamos (Pergamum), Thyatira, Sardis, Philadelphia and Laodicea. First, he acknowledges that the messages Jesus gives to these seven churches were historical in the sense that they were intended for those actual churches at the end of the first century. He believed that their real importance, however, lies in their status as prophecies that reveal the church in every age, from the beginning through the time of the Second Coming of Christ. The seven churches are seven eras. The truth of the gospel has been passed on in each of the eras from church to church, much as a baton is passed from one relay runner to another. The following represents the breakdown of eras of the seven churches:

1. Ephesus (Rev 2:1-7): first and early second century—beginnings

2. Smyrna (Rev 2:8-11): second century to 365—the persecuted church

3. Pergamos (Rev 2:12-17): 365 to the late Middle or Dark Ages—corruption

4. Thyatira (Rev 2:18-29): 1360 to the early seventeenth century—Reformation, survival

5. Sardis (Rev 3:1-6): early seventeenth century to 1931—from England to America

6. Philadelphia (Rev 3:7-13): beginning in 1931—the Armstrong era

7. Laodicea (Rev 3:14-22): the time of the end—corruption and falling away[30]

Armstrong believed that the WCG was presently in the Philadelphia era, the dispensation that would precede Laodicea and the time of the end.

Regarding Armstrong's claim that the WCG was the one true church, we note that this has been echoed by many competing cults and sects whose leaders have made the same claim. Joseph Smith announced that the angel Moroni had revealed to him the truth and that all other denominations were corrupt. Charles Taze Russell taught that the Watchtower Bible and Tract Society was God's true organization on earth. Jim Jones of the People's Temple and David Koresh of the Branch Davidians, along with The Way International, the International Church of Christ and many more cults both past and present, also made or continue to make the claim that they are each the sole proprietor and guardian of the one true faith.

In each instance it is God who has revealed this truth to the cult leader alone. The unfortunate problem that arises, however, is that not only does each of these claims contradict the teachings of traditional Christianity but also they end up contradicting each other. One of the important changes in the new WCG, as we shall see, is that they now acknowledge that there are Christians in other churches besides their own.

Concerning Armstrong's interpretation of the seven churches in Revelation 2 and 3, many Protestant sects and denominations have been strongly influenced by this way of attempting to understand what the Bible teaches about the end of the world. However, Armstrong makes continuous references throughout his reading of these two chapters to the "mark" of the true church. What is this one true mark, which he continues to identify as the guarantee that the church lives on in each successive era? *The keeping of the law*—specifically, strict observance of the sabbath. But if law categories define the church, grace does not. There are few that have matched the WCG as a church governed by law. In fact, during the Armstrong era the WCG showed itself to be among the most qualified among worthy candidates for recognition as a "cult of Christianity."

The Christian church does not use law categories to define itself. The church is described in a number of ways in the Bible. It is the bride of Christ (Rev 19:7; 21:2; 22:17), the assembly of saints (Ps 89:7; Heb 12:23), the body of Christ (Eph 1:23), Christ's church (Mt 16:18), a family in heaven and on earth (Eph 3:15), the flock of God (Is 40:11), God's building (1 Cor 3:9), the temple of God (1 Cor 3:16), the sheep of his pasture (Ps 100:3), a spiritual house (1 Pet 2:5). In the creeds it is the "one, holy, catholic [universal] and apostolic church" and "the communion of saints."

None of these designations for the church alludes to the keeping of the sabbath, or to any law categories whatsoever. They do, however, manifest the language of grace. If indeed the union of husband and wife in holy matrimony is a metaphor for Christ and his church, then how can legalism even be considered in the discussion of a relationship that from the beginning was intended to be built on pure love—the love of God, who in his very essence is love?

As we have seen in this chapter, Armstrong strayed far from the orthodox teachings of Christianity in many areas. We turn in the next chapter to the changes that have taken place as the Worldwide Church of God has encountered the gospel of grace.

FOUR

A Modern-Day Reformation?

Our flawed doctrinal understanding clouded the
plain gospel of Jesus Christ and led to a variety of
wrong conclusions and unscriptural practices. We
have much to repent of and apologize for.
JOSEPH TKACH JR. [1]

O *ne of the distinctives that separated Herbert W. Armstrong from*
many cult leaders was his claim that the Bible was his sole source of
authority and that it would be the Bible from which he would derive his
understanding of doctrine. Charles Taze Russell, founder of the Watchtower Bible and Tract Society, stated that reading the Bible alone would
actually lead Jehovah's Witness believers into darkness; only with the aid
of Russell's *Studies in the Scriptures* could members be assured of a
correct interpretation of the Bible. Mormons look to several books as
authoritative guides to truth, such as the *Book of Mormon, Doctrine and
Covenants* and *Pearl of Great Price,* in addition to the King James Bible.
Many other cults of Christendom use extrabiblical sources of authority to
guide their members.

The Bible Alone—According to Armstrong
Armstrong's claim that the Bible alone led him to what he considered

to be the truth sounds appealing to Protestant Christians. The unorthodox doctrines that Armstrong taught and the WCG espoused, such as Saturday sabbath, Anglo-Israelism, Armstrong's peculiar doctrine on hell, the nature of new birth and observance of the festival days, were said to have been derived from his reading and study of the Bible alone. Yet the claim to stand on Scripture alone, when put into practice by other members of the WCG, eventually became the rope that hung these dogmatic "Armstrongisms" within the church.

In a January 1997 issue of *Worldwide News,* pastor Ted Johnston writes in praise of Armstrong: "Mr. Armstrong imparted to us a great enthusiasm and respect for the Bible. He was eager to defend the reliability and value of all Scripture. He was eager to make the Word of God accessible and meaningful to all people."[2] In actual practice, however, Armstrong's method of looking solely to the Bible to arrive at truth turned out to be *his* sole right, and the Bible was to become "accessible to all people" through Armstrong himself and *his* interpretation of the Bible. In other words, members of the WCG could say they read the Bible to determine truth without the aid of extraneous sources, but in reality any particular interpretations had to agree with Armstrong's views. In the end, this made for no substantial difference in practice between the WCG and other cults of Christianity.

Armstrong, like other cult leaders, believed God had called him to correctly interpret the Word of God for today. He believed this to the end of his life. It was his duty, therefore, to pass his teachings on to the world: "Vistas of knowledge and understanding that have remained the chief mysteries of life to most people were opened to my astonished eyes and mind. But it is recorded in that book that in these very days in which our generation lives, the great mystery would be cleared. And indeed it was to my astonished mind."[3]

The Mantle Is Passed

Armstrong's appointment of Joseph Tkach Sr. to the office of director of church administration in 1979, proved to be an initial impulse toward changes and reforms. Tkach was born in Chicago on March 16, 1927, to first-generation immigrants from Carpatho, Russia. Tkach was raised in the Eastern Orthodox Church, served in the United States

Navy during World War II, and after the war studied at the Illinois Institute of Technology and married Elaine Apostolos. In the 1950s he began reading *The Plain Truth* with great interest. He joined the WCG and was baptized in 1957.

He rose through the ranks rather quickly, as he was ordained a deacon in 1961 and then an elder in 1963. In 1963 he also resigned his career in aviation and began to work full time for the church. In 1966 Tkach moved to Pasadena to join the church's Ambassador College staff. In 1974 he became a local church elder; in 1979 he was appointed director of ministerial services. In 1981 he was handpicked by Armstrong to serve on the board of directors, and in 1985 Armstrong named him the second pastor general of the WCG. Armstrong died in 1986. A new era had begun in the history of the WCG.

The motivation for Tkach's initiation of change and reform certainly seems to have been his desire to follow the guiding light of Scripture. Ruth Tucker, visiting professor at Trinity Evangelical Divinity School and well-published author on cults, poignantly remarks that this "can be a dangerous approach for a sectarian group."[4]

The first reforms under Tkach were not monumental, however, compared to what would take place later under the leadership of his son, Joseph Tkach Jr. As a matter of fact, the loyalty Tkach felt toward his predecessor is quite apparent in the support and publication of "18 Truths," shortly after Armstrong's death. Wrote Tkach:

> The Editorial Services staff has compiled here, for the first time in any of the Church's publications, 18 essential, basic truths that God restored to his Church through our late Pastor General Herbert W. Armstrong. As you prepare spiritually for the coming Feast of Tabernacles, please spend time with this important article, reviewing each of the eighteen truths and thanking God for restoring them to His Church.[5]

The eighteen items included in list form had to do with the following:

1. The government of God.
2. The gospel of the kingdom of God.
3. The purpose of God.
4. Who and what is God?
5. What is man?

6. The human spirit in man.

7. The church is only the firstfruits.

8. The church is not yet the kingdom of God.

9. Only those whom God the Father calls and draws to him can be converted now.

10. The resurrection to judgment.

11. The millennium.

12. The Holy Spirit coming into us only begets us.

13. We are only begotten now, not born again.

14. The identity of modern Israel.

15. Prophecy can be understood only if you know that we are the Israelites.

16. The annual festivals.

17. The authority of the sacred calendar, preserved by the Jews.

18. Second and third tithe.

This list indicates, of course, that Tkach was still very much a supporter of Armstrong's "trespasses" for which his son would be making a plea of forgiveness for one decade later.

David Neff writes:

One of the first doctrines to be questioned after Armstrong's death was his teaching that believers were not born again until the resurrection. Re-examining that teaching in the light of Scripture led the WCG leaders (who seem to function as a team) to reject their church's teaching that human beings were themselves destined to become gods, which in turn, led them to teach the Biblical doctrine of the Holy Trinity. "It was a domino effect," they recently told CT *[Christianity Today]*.[6]

Law and Grace

The issue that sparked the greatest controversy in the WCG was not what it means to be born again, Anglo-Israelism or even the Trinity. The concern that became most controversial in the WCG was actually the same, in many respects, as the question the early church faced when St. Paul was asked to appear at the Jerusalem Council in Acts 15.

In fact it is an issue that has been brought up time and again throughout the history of the Christian church: the matter of grace and law. The question becomes, How does one obtain right standing with God? As Paul battled for free and justifying grace, he insisted that Gentile Christians need not be burdened with Jewish ceremonial laws. He takes up this issue ferociously in his epistles to the Romans and the Galatians. As one theologian once put it, "Galatians is where St. Paul fought the battle of grace. Romans was the mop-up action."

St. Augustine (354-430) took the baton from St. Paul in his opposition to Pelagius in the fourth century. Pelagius taught that an individual can take the first step toward salvation through his or her own free will, apart from grace. The Pelagian controversy caused Augustine to reflect deeply on the meaning of grace and free will, and he wrote vehemently against Pelagianism. The church recognized that Pelagius was in error at the Council of Carthage in 418.

Martin Luther (1493-1546), an Augustinian monk, took up the battle in the sixteenth century and challenged the whole of Western Christendom on the issue of grace and works. Luther insisted that we are not saved by our own deeds or works of the law. It is Christ's righteousness alone that is sufficient for salvation. Luther's strong leadership and courage brought about the Protestant Reformation on the principles of *sola Scriptura, sola fide* and *sola gratia* (the Bible alone, faith alone, and grace alone). John Calvin, the French-Swiss Reformer advocated these same views of grace.

For Protestants this is an old issue. However, the grace/works controversy has become the most important discussion in the WCG today. The story is particularly interesting because the WCG is currently attempting to fit within the mainstream of broad-based evangelicalism, certainly one of the important byproducts of the Reformation.

We have demonstrated that Herbert W. Armstrong did not understand or teach the gospel of justification by grace through faith apart from the works of the law. At the very least, he mingled elements of grace and law so extensively that any resemblance of the gospel he might have hit upon quickly dissipated in a legalistic quagmire.

The present leadership of the WCG is wrestling in earnest with Armstrong's understanding of the gospel. In our interviews in the appendices, the reader will note that the WCG still attempts to argue that Armstrong really did teach the good news that Jesus justifies sinners through his shed blood and death on the cross. In light of the WCG's present teachings concerning the gospel, this conclusion is somewhat surprising. We have carefully reviewed many of Armstrong's writings, and we conclude that his teachings about the gospel do not approximate what is now being taught in the church that he founded.

Some critics insist that Armstrong really understood the gospel in a millennial sense—that is, identifying it as belonging to the coming kingdom of God. William Meyer, a former member of the WCG, sees a striking resemblance between the old WCG and the Judaizers Paul opposes in his epistle to the Galatians. Citing several commentaries, Meyer qualifies his position by stating:

> The Galatian opponents and the old WCG did not actually teach "legalism" or salvation by works. Instead, they and the old WCG taught a "covenantal nomism" which is similar to what Orthodox, normative Judaism teaches. Covenantal nomism (see Richard Longenecker, *Word Biblical Commentary: Galatians,* pp. 86, 95, 96) teaches that one needs God's mercy, B-U-T, because we receive God's mercy, we must also keep God's law. In the case of the Galatian opponent, this involved Jewish boundary markers of circumcision, food rules, and Hebraic holy days. . . . Paul . . . is not really attacking legalism per se, which very few believed or taught in its pure form then or now. He is attacking a nomism, which boils down at the end of the day, to the equivalent of legalism.
>
> Remove circumcision from the covenantal nomism of the circumcision party, and the teaching Paul attacks in Galatians is basically identical with the official teaching of the old WCG and its conservative splinter groups today. This is why Galatians is so antagonistic and dangerous to the classic theology of Armstrongism.[7]

This issue continues to divide the WCG. While the splinter groups who are loyal to Armstrong continue to argue that the WCG has tragically forsaken Armstrong, some detractors argue that the WCG has not moved far enough. Joseph Tkach Jr. told us that the concern is really not with Armstrong's understanding of the gospel. The real concern has to do with making changes far more quickly than the membership can absorb. To denounce Armstrong would not be prudent or necessary, because he was the founder of their church and is therefore an important part of the WCG's identity.

Dialogue Opens

When Armstrong died in 1986, many members of the WCG became disillusioned. HWA was Elijah, the embodiment of all that was true about the WCG. Some of the most steadfast members even gathered at his grave to await what they believed would be his resurrection before the return of Jesus Christ. For a majority of the flock, however, it was time to move on. After all, Armstrong had named Tkach as his successor. This must mean, many concluded, that the mantle had now been passed from Elijah to Elisha.

On the whole, members were willing to switch loyalties to the new administration. As noted above, Tkach did not make any major changes at first, and with the publication of the "18 Truths" and the republication of several of Armstrong's books, it seemed as if the new administration was indeed carrying the mantle of the founder of the church.

A current leader of the WCG told us candidly that in the immediate months following Armstrong's death, a feeling of mistrust filled the air at headquarters in Pasadena. Armstrong's iron will and demand for unquestioning obedience had bred fear among his immediate staff that prevented effective, wholesome and honest communication among them. Gregory Albrecht, senior editor of *The Plain Truth,* told us that he had trouble trusting anyone at the headquarters for a number of years after Armstrong's death.

In our third interview, Pastor General Joseph Tkach Jr. and Gregory Albrecht spoke freely about the changes that led to the present situation. As they began to learn to trust one another in the new spirit of openness permitted by Joseph Tkach Sr., more and more theological issues began to surface for discussion.

David Covington, who is now an ex-member (see next chapter), recalls being in a "Doctrines of the WCG" class in 1990 when arguments about the nature of Jesus and God were being explored by one of his Ambassador College professors, Dr. Donald Ward. Further discussion ensued with Dr. K. J. Stavrinides, a respected Bible scholar, along with another scholar,

Dr. Hoch. Soon many of the staff were engaged in active, open dialogue about numerous doctrines. This new spirit of openness and trust greatly contributed to the important changes that have taken place in the past several years.

According to Joseph Tkach Jr., the doctrine of God really served as the catalyst for all the later changes. After a Roman Catholic priest responded to an antitrinitarian letter printed in *The Plain Truth,* Mike Feazell, assistant to the pastor general, began to study the doctrine with Stavrinides. Feazell and his assistant C. W. Davis had also been attending Azusa Pacific University to further their studies in theology. At Azusa, Feazell realized that the WCG needed to make some specific changes, and he began to press Tkach in that direction. The studies led by Stavrinides and Hoeh brought more and more people "into the loop," as Tkach puts it. The leaders, he says, simply kept yielding to the Holy Spirit as changes began to take place. The pace of change quickened after 1993.[8]

Still, many of these discussions were confined to headquarters in Pasadena. Changes at the top were not being communicated clearly to the membership or to the pastors in the hundreds of churches. By the time the changes were disseminated to the church body as a whole, they were more or less already officially adopted or assumed to be true. This has led to confusion and anger and has resulted in some membership losses.

Questions and Conflicts

In the November and December 1993 issues of *Reviews You Can Use,* a WCG ministerial journal, an Atlanta pastor named Earl Williams published an article titled "Are We Saved by Baptism?" Williams called into question Armstrong's teaching that baptism is an ordinance that must be obeyed in order for one to receive salvation. His ideas caused some stir.

In January 1994 *The Plain Truth* carried another article by Williams, "Homes," about Habitat for Humanity. In it Williams showed his willingness to stretch beyond the boundaries of the WCG: "The message of Habitat is: Jesus Christ can make a difference in people through you."[9] *The Worldwide News* of June 1994 carried yet another essay in which Williams's views became clearer. In "Which Church Is God's True Church?" he made a daring claim that would have never been articulated, much less discussed, in a WCG publication if Armstrong had been alive. Williams contended that *there are Christians in other churches.* "Which church is God's?" he asked. Quoting from Paul's letter to the Ephesians, he maintained, "Paul does not mention any denomination or human organization. The church of God is therefore the Body of Christ."[10] By stating that there are Christians in other churches, Williams contradicted Armstrong's teaching that the WCG is God's only true organization on earth.

Even if the leaders in Pasadena had come to agree with Williams, the majority of WCG members still held to Armstrong's teaching. After the June 1994 article, letters and phone calls of protest flooded in. The *Worldwide News* staff asked Williams to write an article stating what "he did not mean" to say when he wrote previously, but he refused. *The Worldwide News* quickly republished a previous pastor general's report dated March 30, 1993, which said in part, "The rumor that has been circulated is that we now believe all churches are God's churches. That is most certainly not our belief." Yet Joseph Tkach Sr. himself no longer believed that the WCG was the one true church.

Current leaders report that Joseph Tkach Sr. had begun to reflect on this issue shortly after Armstrong appointed him to be the new pastor general. Recently his son, Joseph Tkach Jr., recalled in an interview, "My dad, the first couple of years after he was our denominational leader, couldn't help but think of the notion previously taught by our church—that there are no other Christians, that we're the one and only true church—and find himself quite bothered by that."[11]

This raises a question. Some years after Tkach's rethinking of the issue, when Earl Williams stated that there were Christians in other churches, why was he urged to retract or at least explain "what he didn't mean"? As early as December 1990, the public relations spokesman for the WCG had stated in an interview that "the WCG does not consider itself to be the exclusive representation of the body of Christ."[12]

Here is one possible explanation. Changes in thinking at headquarters were not being effectively communicated to the church at large. It was only when one of the local pastors became vocal that the issues became controversial among the general membership. Evidently Tkach, in the interests of keeping the church on an even keel, remained circumspect. He was well aware that given his position, what he said about any issue would be weighed very carefully. Williams, on the other hand, was not constrained by such pressures, and having a pulpit to preach from and a sizable congregation to listen, he had been proclaiming for months those things that he believed to be true. He no longer believed the old Armstrongisms. Yet he was ministering in a denomination that by and large still did. Many were simply not accepting the changes. This left Tkach in a quandary. After all, he was the leader of a whole church, not just one congregation. How would he respond in the midst of what could well turn out to be a major crisis? A meeting between the pastor general and Earl Williams seemed imminent.

To further complicate the issue, Williams was now openly attacking Armstrong's sacred cow, the sabbath. He denied that sabbath observance was required for salvation and was preaching and emphasizing the grace of God in and through the death and resurrection of Jesus Christ. Williams was also preaching against the legitimacy of the holy days. He contended that Armstrong's teachings concerning the sabbath were the epitome of works righteousness over and against the New Testament's emphasis on grace and grace alone as sufficient for salvation.

In a phone interview Williams told us that he had experienced a conversion and had been "born again" in 1989. He did not mean what Armstrong had meant by that. According to Williams, his new birth was the experience of knowing Jesus Christ and being unshackled from the heavy yoke of the law which had long burdened him under Armstrong. As he continued to proclaim grace, he said, he had earned the reputation of being "the grace preacher." He stressed the importance of experiencing the grace of God, not just talking about it, which he believes is what is going on in the WCG today.

A Point of Crisis
Things came to a head in the fall of 1994 at the WCG's Feast of

Tabernacles in Daytona, Florida. There David Hulme, then the WCG director of communications, preached a sermon on the importance of keeping the law the way Armstrong had taught it should be kept. Two days later, Earl Williams preached on the all-sufficiency of grace. Hulme asked Tkach for permission to renounce Williams publicly. The request was denied. Tkach admonished Williams to preach on other subjects until the problem could be addressed by the church. Williams refused and simply continued to preach grace. On December 18, 1994, Joseph Tkach Sr. flew to Atlanta to meet with Earl Williams and address the many members who were sharply divided over grace and law.

Arriving in Atlanta, Tkach found that among the fifteen hundred members in attendance to hear him, things had gotten so volatile that half of the crowd were threatening to walk out if he preached law. The other half would do the same if he preached grace. Williams had met with Tkach the previous night and told him it was his intention to resign from ministry in the WCG. Tkach implored him to remain, which he agreed to do, at least temporarily.

For now, wisdom dictated that Tkach take a moderate approach in order to placate both sides before any rash judgments caused a split in the church. The WCG would recommend that members continue to observe the sabbath, but no longer would it be considered a standard by which to judge other Christians. Tkach published what he called his "new covenant" proclamation (see "The Sabbath" in appendix one). Despite his caution, his statement added to the growing tension in the WCG, chiefly among those who were not in favor of the reforms coming out of Pasadena and those who opposed Williams's grace ministry.

It was in 1995 that the dam burst in the WCG, bringing a flurry of activity and change throughout the organization. A storm of protests from both pastors and laypeople rained on Pasadena. Resignations were offered everywhere. One of those resigning was David Hulme, who accused Tkach of having deceived the WCG by accepting Armstrong's appointment as pastor general at a time when he already believed doctrines he knew were contrary to Armstrong's teachings. Earl Williams also submitted his final resignation in March 1995.

In the midst of the controversy, Joseph Tkach Sr. was diagnosed with cancer in early 1995; he succumbed to it on September 23, 1995, at the age of sixty-eight. Tkach will be remembered as a leader who took the WCG into a new era and was forced to navigate storms of great controversy and change.

Momentum for Transformation

Joseph Tkach Jr. was born in Chicago on December 3, 1951. Because of his father's work with the WCG, he moved to Pasadena in 1966; there he completed high school at Imperial, the WCG's K-12 educational program. He entered Ambassador College in 1969 and graduated in 1973 with a bachelor's degree in theology. Later he earned an M.B.A. at Western International University in Phoenix, Arizona. He served in a salaried ministerial post for a short time in the WCG and was laid off along with approximately forty others. Then Tkach spent briefly (1976-1977) at the Arizona Boys Ranch, where his responsibilities included developing rehabilitation programs for juvenile delinquents. From 1977 to 1984 he worked for the state of Arizona as a social worker, handling cases for the developmentally disabled. He was employed by Intel Corporation between 1984 and 1986, serving as a trainer in the corporate services department.

Like his father, Joe Tkach Jr. never pastored a congregation. He did serve as a local church elder after his graduation—an unpaid position in a local church under a senior pastor. Joe Tkach married Tamara (Tammy) Hall in 1980. They have two children, Joseph Tkach III and Stephanie. In 1986 the Tkachs moved back to Pasadena, where Joseph Tkach Jr. became the director of church administration, replacing his father at the time Joe Tkach Sr. became WCG's pastor general. When his father died in 1995, Joe Tkach Jr. in turn was appointed pastor general of the Worldwide Church of God.

FIVE

Reactions

There is only one thing in the world
worse than being talked about,
and that is not being talked about.
OSCAR WILDE

A *work of this nature would not be complete unless it covered overall* reactions to the developments in the last eleven years in the WCG. As we mentioned earlier, when we published our first book on the cults in 1993, one former WCG leader (who has asked to remain unnamed) contacted George, commending us for acknowledging the changes that the WCG was already undergoing. We had not been able to document the response as fully as we would have liked, however, because at the time we finished writing that book the changes were still too new. But there have been many reactions to the changes in the WCG since then.

Some reactions from within the church have been deeply moving. A woman from Virginia reports:

I spent 27 years in the WCG, my husband just over 10. We left in 1991. One of the struggles we have faced is a strong wariness of "organization." At first we did not want to be affiliated with a church. And, it seems, relationships are harder in some ways. Before we had the common bond of having our beliefs dictated to us. Now it is unlikely that we will find anyone who believes exactly the same as we do on every issue. I also felt my credibility was lessened because I had been in a cult.

The most helpful part of our journey has been a relationship with the Holy Spirit.[1]

A Florida woman tells her feelings about her involvement for thirteen years in the WCG:

The main struggle I faced when I left was what WCG members would think of me. We were told that when someone left the WCG they lost their crown, and in my mind, were "exterminated for eternity."

I relate healing with my Savior Jesus Christ, who delivers me and others from what I found to be the confines of the WCG. . . .

Leaving the WCG might be very painful, but it has been such a blessing for me personally.[2]

Significant reactions to the Tkach administrations come from three categories of people. First, some groups, because of continued loyalty to Armstrong, have splintered from the WCG. These groups view the new changes as outright betrayals of what they regard to be the pure teachings of Herbert W. Armstrong.

Second, the evangelical community has largely come to embrace the WCG and welcome the organization as a legitimate denomination within Christianity.

Third are those members who have left the Worldwide Church of God altogether, not because they have a continued loyalty for Armstrong as the splinter groups do but because they believe that the current administration has not gone far enough in reforming Armstrongism. Some of these have been and continue to be vocal in their dissent. Many ex-members have gone on to join conventional Christian churches, either as pastors or as laypersons. Many of them are attempting to rebuild their lives. More than a few are disillusioned and for one reason or another have continued to absent themselves from organized religion.

The Splinter Groups

The period of 1993-1995 proved to be a trying time in the WCG. Many changes were taking place now, and as they began to escalate, shock waves moved among the entire membership. When word came that substantial changes were taking place, significant numbers reacted by reverting to the security and stability of Armstrongism. Three major splinter groups and several lesser ones broke away from the WCG, all more or less espousing the traditional theology of Armstrong. Note that these more recent splinter groups broke away because of their *loyalty to* Armstrong, while the groups that broke away in the 1970s and early 1980s were started by former members who opposed him.

The first major group to voice protest over the changes in Pasadena and actually break away was the Philadelphia Church of God. It is headed by Gerald Flurry, along with John Amos in Edmond, Oklahoma. Flurry, a devotee of Armstrong, was "fired" by the Tkach administration because of his "disagreement with the new direction" Armstrong's successor was taking the church, according *The Philadelphia Trumpet,* the church's news publication. Flurry and about a dozen other Armstrong devotees launched the Philadelphia Church of God on the sabbath of December 16, 1989. After several months the new movement had about thirty-five members. At the time of our writing, the Philadelphia church boasts five to six thousand members worldwide. It also has a television ministry that appears on seventy stations worldwide.

Flurry is perhaps the purest representation of Armstrongism. He believes that Armstrong was the "endtime Elijah" of the Bible's prophecies. He accuses Pasadena of making over forty changes in the teachings of Armstrong. He has published a strongly worded pamphlet titled *WCG Doctrinal Changes and the Tragic Results.* Flurry follows Armstrong as closely to the letter as can be imagined. The Philadelphia church retains the doctrines of Anglo-Israelism, keeping the sabbath as a condition of salvation, baptism as a necessity for salvation, and other teachings that characterized the founder of the WCG.

The Global Church of God formed in 1990 and is based in San Diego, California. Roderick Meredith, Armstrong's former biographer, is the leader of this movement, which boasts seven thousand members to date. Meredith continues to uphold the doctrine of British Israelism, and the group is very authoritarian in its polity. Along with

Meredith, another leader of the movement is Raymond McNair. Periodicals include *World Ahead Magazine* and *Global Church News*.

The United Church of God was formed at a conference in Indianapolis in May 1995. David Hulme was named chairman of the board. By the beginning of 1996, the newly formed United Church had attracted over seventeen thousand members, thus proving the greatest threat to the WCG. It is estimated at this time that the United Church of God will also attract over one hundred pastors who were previously part of the WCG. Hulme, together with Bob Dick, heads up the United Church of God with headquarters in Arcadia, California. The movement publishes *Good News* magazine, which continues to focus on holy days, the sabbath, the law and other Armstrong themes. The United Church of God elects its president and practices collaborative church government.

Smaller groups that have broken away from the WCG include Church of the Great God (1992), Twentieth Century Church of God (1990—not to be confused with the 1974 group with the same name), the United Biblical Church of God (1992) and Triumph Prophetic Ministries (1987). All these splinter groups attempt to promote Armstrongism to varying degrees, in reaction to what is considered the tragic betrayal in Pasadena.

There were approximately 350 pastors in the WCG as of early 1995. More than 40 percent of them either have resigned since that time or have been terminated. There are currently about 254 WCG pastors in the United States, pastoring approximately 420 congregations in all fifty states and the District of Columbia.

Evangelicalism

News of the doctrinal changes in the WCG has spread throughout evangelical Christendom, and responses have been varied. As observed in the previous chapter, many evangelicals have welcomed the WCG with open arms. Others are a bit more cautious. Needless to say, the WCG has been delighted with the warm embrace that evangelical leaders have given them. The March/April 1997 edition of *The Plain Truth* features Billy Graham, the icon of evangelicalism, on its front cover. This is highly symbolic of where the WCG perceives itself to be heading and how it has attempted to position itself as a legitimate part of the evangelical community.

The WCG has been keenly aware of the various cult watch groups that publish literature about it. In 1992 Publishers of Biblical Literature, with headquarters in Braine l'Alleud, Belgium, received a letter from David Hulme asking for changes and corrections in a 1985 booklet titled *Insights into Armstrongism.* In an article published in February 1993 in the bulletin *Le Messager Evangelique* (the evangelical messenger), the author, Christian Piette, responded most positively to Hulme's request. Piette writes, "Is not this cause for rejoicing? Followers of *La Pure Verité (The Plain Truth)* have moved from the position of a sect, to that of a denomination. We want to encourage them to continue along that road."

Many of the changes prior to 1993 took place without significant media coverage. This changed in 1995, when press coverage started to explode and numerous evangelical periodicals featured news reports and interviews on the WCG's transformation. Following are some of the statements made in prominent evangelical publications about the changes that have come to the WCG.

Christian Research Journal, Spring/Summer 1994: "One group that has profited from continued dialogue with evangelicals is the Worldwide Church of God (WCG), which has now been declared doctrinally sound by many experts" (Joe Maxwell, "Cult Watchers See Troubling Trends").

The Council of Chalcedon, April 1995: "It seems as though we must rejoice over such unprecedented developments and welcome them as brethren, praying that the Lord will continue to move powerfully in their midst. Hallelujah! Glory be to God! Here may well be one of the 'kingdoms of the world' that has become part of the Kingdom of our Lord and of His Christ" (Dewey H. Hodges, "Acknowledging the Plain Truth").

Christianity Today, October 2, 1995: "But how will we respond? Sadly Christians outside the WCG have been suspicious and slow to extend the right hand of fellowship. (A few leaders have been helpful, WCG leaders say . . .) CT commends the WCG leadership for its courage in pursuit of truth. Can we now welcome their people into this transdenominational fellowship we call evangelicalism?" (David Neff, "The Road to Orthodoxy").

Christian Research Journal, Winter 1996: In a journalistic "Newswatch" piece called "The Worldwide Church of God: Resurrected into Orthodoxy," the author, Doug LeBlanc, does not attempt to draw any conclusions himself but reports the conclusions of others. He does state, "Unlike the days of Herbert Armstrong, the doors of most WCG churches are now open to visitors, and WCG leaders are thinking about what they can contribute to their newly discovered Christian brothers and sisters in other churches." This issue of the CRI journal also features an article by Joseph Tkach Jr. himself, in which he recalls the events of the previous ten years.

Sower, Winter 1996 (a publication of the Bible Society in Australia): In what surely must be one of the greatest ironies of our time, the organization which for decades published *The Plain Truth* has discovered the plain truth about the gospel of Jesus Christ.

The Worldwide Church of God (WCG) . . . has been in the midst of profound change—all because one man, Joseph W. Tkach, Pastor General of the Worldwide Church of God, studied the Bible with an open mind. ("The Bible Reveals Plain Truth")

Christian Research Journal, Winter/Spring 1996: A one-page article titled "New Beginning, New Leadership for the Worldwide Church of God" refers the reader back to the Winter 1996 issue (see above). Additionally it says: "Once the WCG began heeding God's Word, there was no turning back, and its commitment to Scripture above expediency has exacted a staggering price in defections and lost income."

Charisma, July 1996:

A search for biblical truth has led to a spiritual awakening within an organization formerly considered a cult. Leaders of the Worldwide Church of God (WCG) . . . have publicly recanted teachings that set them apart from orthodox Christianity.

Joseph Tkach Jr., the group's president, gives the Holy Spirit full credit for the awakening. He said WCG leaders recognized contradictions between Armstrong's teaching and Scripture. (Anahid Schweikert, "Former Cult Embraces Bible Doctrines")

Christianity Today, July 15, 1996:

The turnaround in this movement shows how hungry people are for an authentic Christian gospel. The legalism that characterizes so many of the cultic and sectarian movements—and segments of the evangelical church—simply does not satisfy people spiritually.

Likewise, the broader Christian community would do well to take note of the vitality of faith that is so evident in this church. Pastors and lay-Christians alike are digging into the Bible to check out this "new covenant" teaching for themselves. (Ruth Tucker, "From the Fringe to the Fold: How the Worldwide Church of God Discovered the Plain Truth of the Gospel")

Cornerstone, Winter 1997:

But unlike any previous countercult article *Cornerstone* has published, the story of the Worldwide Church of God is not a story with a tragic ending. Instead, the WCG today is a church in every sense of the word. Make that "Word." The journey toward orthodoxy began in 1986, after the death of Herbert W. Armstrong. Joseph W. Tkach Sr. took over the reins of the WCG as its Pastor General, and almost immediately, cracks began to appear in the foundation of Armstrongism. Though the elder Tkach died in September of 1995, his son Joseph, along with other leaders, continued dismantling Armstrong's doctrine in favor of Biblical orthodoxy. ("The Saga of a Cult Gone Good")

Religious Broadcasting, February/March 1997:

What are we to say to all this? How should we respond? How does the flock respond when the shepherd reaches out to locate and rescue his lost sheep?

Some may suggest that there is a subtle effort afoot to counterweight the Gospel and confuse unwitting believers. Some have already responded to this wonderful news by saying that the Worldwide Church of God is trying to pull the wool over the eyes of the flock. . . .

I am thrilled and delighted to personally know the leadership of the Worldwide Church of God. . . .

The Worldwide Church of God needs to tell its story. *The Plain Truth* needs to thrive and grow in influence as it stands for the kind of reformation that leads to revival and growth in the body of Christ. . . .

With the courageous, uncompromising stance of the Worldwide Church of God, dedicated to proclaiming the message of God's all-sufficient grace in Jesus Christ, the honest-to-God plain truth can be clearly shouted from the housetops!

Please join me in welcoming our new brothers and sisters in the Lord. (Richard C. Dean, "Open Arms: Welcoming the Worldwide Church of God")

Footprints, January 20, 1997 (a newsletter of the Evangelical Christian Publishers Association, or ECPA):

What are the top stories of 1996? It is interesting to read the selected items for "religion"; quite often they are representative of problems rather than victories.

Let me tell you what I think is the TOP RELIGIOUS STORY OF 1996.

It is the announcement, clarification, and progress in the faith journey of THE WORLDWIDE CHURCH OF GOD. It is the joining of Plain Truth Ministries with magazines and publishers who previously denounced them as a cult. It is the conversion and repentance story of the leadership of this movement.

The Bible tells us that "angels rejoice in heaven over one sinner that repents."

Can you imagine the noise in heaven over the salvation of a movement?

Let's continue to rejoice too as we increase our fellowship with these new children of God.

Most recent articles in evangelical periodicals include the praise of important leaders. A warm reception has been given to the WCG by several faculty from Azusa Pacific University, Ruth Tucker from Trinity Evangelical Divinity School, and Rev. Bill Brafford, a pastoral spokesman from the Four Square Gospel tradition, as well as the Four Square denominational leader, Dr. John Holland. A number of people in our denomination, the Lutheran Church Missouri Synod, have joined in the welcome. These include the president of the LCMS, Al Barry, whom Tkach and Albrecht warmly refer to as "big Al, the preacher's pal." Others in the Missouri Synod contingent are Jerald Joerz, Roger Pitelko, Robert Dargartz, Rod Rosenblatt, Charles Manske (founder of Concordia University in Irvine, California), Kent Puls, Steve Mueller, Paul McCain (who arranged the meeting) and the two of us.[3] Another LCMS Lutheran, Don Mazat from Jubilee Network, conducted an interview in which he lauded the progress of the WCG as they have moved toward orthodoxy.

Hendrik (Hank) Hanegraaff, the current president of Christian Research Institute, has affirmed the WCG in his radio broadcasts on the popular *The Bible Answer Man,* in articles published in *Christian Research Journal* and in interviews and public statements. Ruth Tucker makes note of a statement made by Hanegraaff on *The Bible Answer Man:* "Rather than developing hurdles for these guys to jump over, our job is to facilitate the process." Tucker writes further: "In an recent radio interview with Tkach, Jr., and Albrecht, Hanegraaff introduced them as 'brothers in the Lord.' "[4]

Joseph Tkach Jr. later reflected on Hanegraaff's warm embrace: "When we came out of the cave, what we found was that some of the cult-watching groups made the journey ten times more difficult. Hank was one who was not that way. Hank was gracious. Hank welcomed us. Hank encouraged us."[5]

An important voice in the more conservative Presbyterian branch of evangelicalism is D. James Kennedy, pastor of Coral Ridge Presbyterian Church, who reported that the WCG phenomenon is "the most astonishing change that I have ever seen or heard of in any religious group, for which I, for one, praise God."[6] In a letter dated May 15, 1997, of which Joseph Tkach furnished us a copy, Kennedy wrote to Mike Dutko of the WCG in response to a letter outlining polity and other problems the WCG faces. Kennedy's response in part is as follows:

> The extensive theological reforms which have taken place in this church are without precedent in church history. They are vastly more extensive than even the Protestant Reformation. I feel confident that in time these inherent pressures will work toward a more democratic and republican government. Your church has been through some extraordinarily rough waters. My advice would be to thank God for what has happened and trust Him for complete reformation in the future. In about one decade, your organization

has been changed from a cult to a church. This has never, to my knowledge, happened before in church history.

The Voices of Dissent

Not surprisingly, the harshest reactions have come from ex-members and reform-minded splinter groups that have broken away in recent years. There is no way of knowing for sure how many people are included in this third category. Millions once subscribed to *The Plain Truth.* That readership is now down to about 125,000. In December 1996 an article by Pastor General Tkach in *The Worldwide News* stated that since 1990, forty thousand people have left the WCG without joining one of the splinter groups. Acknowledging that these former members are confused, angry and hurting, Tkach invited them to consider returning to the WCG because the church now has corrected the wrongs that caused the hurt in the first place.

Dissenters include former members who have devoted themselves to ministries that reach out to ex-members through mail, personal contact, newsletters and so on. Much of the communication takes place over the Internet. In the bibliography we list some of the web sites we have used.

David Covington, an ex-member who pastored several WCG congregations and wrote for *The Plain Truth,* has a newsletter called *Crossroads* that he says is devoted to helping and providing support for ex-members who have been hurt by involvement with the WCG. Covington is a personal friend and apologist of Earl Williams and had been a lifelong member of WCG until he left. He reports that he attempted to remain with the church for as long as possible and maintained a successful ministry even in the troubled times.

Covington's resignation from the church came only after he realized, as he strongly insists, that the leaders were not sincere, were exploitive, still want to hang on to Armstrong and have not really considered the substance and significance of Earl Williams's grace ministry. He says they refuse to consider reorganizing the movement and changing the bylaws so as to establish and maintain accountability; they have not opened financial records or published the salaries of present administrators. Covington says the church leaders persist in what he calls abusive treatment of many current WCG ministers. We brought the criticisms that Covington and others like him to Tkach, Gregory Albrecht and Mike Feazell; their responses are included in this book's appendices.

Along with other dissenters, Covington is disappointed with evangelicalism's warm, seemingly uncritical embrace of the WCG. He wonders why many in the evangelical camp have not asked hard questions but have simply and openly placed their stamp of approval on all that has allegedly transpired in the movement in the last ten years.

Those who were closest to the crisis in the WCG, its ex-members, are the ones who have been most affected by the changes—or what they perceive to be the lack thereof. Prominent evangelicals, on the other hand, have been encountering general news of the changes, particularly in key doctrines such as the Trinity, Jesus Christ and the significance of grace. Evangelicals have not been personally attached to WCG group dynamics as were the ex-members. This can be good, as it has allowed them to judge the WCG strictly on the basis of doctrinal statements rather than on more subjective factors such as salaries and personality conflicts. In other words, evangelical concern is directed to the content of WCG theology, not so much to people involved in the organization's past. Consequently, these disenfranchised are still struggling to find a theological home.

SIX

From the Outside
Looking In

*The law is only a shadow
of the good things that are coming.*
HEBREWS 10:1

*T*he story of the WCG has indeed been a compelling one. *Writing*
as outsiders has proved to have both advantages and disadvantages.
The obvious advantage has been that we believe we have been able to
maintain a fair degree of objectivity, simply because we have not been
a direct part of the emotional ethos of the organization, as are many
persons whose lives have been directly affected as leaders, members
and ex-members. On the other hand, perhaps as outsiders we lack a
passion that may very well be necessary to understand the dynamics
of the narrative.

When retrieving the daily mail, one quickly sifts through the items
and lays those marked "bulk rate" aside. We would rather read instead
the mail that bears our name written in ink, with a postage stamp
attached. We hope our account will not be assessed as "bulk rate." We
do not think it will be, simply because we *have* participated in ongoing
theological reflection with WCG's leaders and former members. We

hope that as part of the church that came out of the Reformation, we can be of some ongoing assistance, particularly since the WCG is presently seeking to define itself in terms of justification by grace through faith, the very doctrine that was the central focus of the Reformation. We also hope we may be able to aid the WCG in understanding the importance of the doctrine of the church itself.

This final chapter is being written as I (Larry Nichols) travel through Russia by train on the trans-Siberian railroad from Ekaterinburg to Novosebirsk, where the Lutheran Church Missouri Synod will be dedicating a seminary called Concordia Theological College. Gazing out the window at the green landscape of the Siberian plain, dotted by clusters of birch trees and occasional dilapidated villages, I remember the week past.

Several professors at our seminary and I just completed a series of lectures to theological students struggling to form a Lutheran mission here in the former Soviet Union. At our opening worship I was deeply moved as I listened to the Russian young people sing the liturgy and openly profess their faith in a country that for seventy years had made every effort to stamp out Christianity. I thought of the glorious words of our Lord Jesus Christ, "The gates of hell shall not prevail against my church" (see Mt 16:18). Those words rang powerfully in my mind as I realized that the church lives on under the most oppressive of conditions.

And then my mind drifted back to the task at hand. I realized that the WCG was under its own Babylonian captivity for an almost equal number of decades. It is truly remarkable to see the grace of God emerging in the lives of many people who endured many years in the shackles of legalism.

Questions of Accountability

At the time of this writing (July 1997), Pastor General Joseph Tkach Jr. is in the process of publishing his own book telling the story of the WCG from the inside. His work will be called *Transformed by Truth.* He showed us the table of contents, and it is evident that he is making every effort to assess the changes in the WCG. The titles of the chapters indicate that he is addressing the issues and concerns that have been raised by those who have opposed the events of the last eleven years. No doubt more books will be generated as the story of the WCG continues to unfold in the years ahead. There are a number of concerns we hope Tkach and his fellow leaders will address.

Accountability is an important issue for the WCG. In our third meeting Tkach told us that people have been accusing the WCG of lacking accountability, accusing him of appointing "dummy boards." He readily acknowledges that under Armstrong this was certainly true. But he insisted that the lack of accountability that characterized the Armstrong era has been remedied.

The church, he said, can never go back to the old ways; he listed three basic ways the WCG is moving toward total accountability. First, the bylaws are being revised; the changes are to be established within the next several years, and thereafter a board of directors will be independently appointed.

Second, the WCG is working on a statement of ethics and accountability that will greatly improve the WCG's polity. On this second point, we hope that such a document will be based not on law but gospel. Most evangelical churches use 1 Timothy 3:1-13 as an adequate model for the determining the qualifications of a minister of the gospel and the ethical guidelines such a minister should follow.

Third, Tkach stated that the WCG is a "people's movement." "The majority of the people who are members of the WCG," he insisted, "simply would not permit the organization to revert back to the days of Armstrongism."

We encourage the WCG to move in the direction of the accountability that must always be in place in the Christian church. We also hope that detractors and critics of the WCG will follow Martin Luther's explanation of the eighth commandment about "bearing false witness" (ninth commandment in the Reformed tradition): that we are called to "put the best construction on everything." If the WCG needs time to make important changes, we hope they will be afforded it.

The episcopal polity, which the present administration claims to be its own, is certainly a legitimate one, as the Roman Catholic, Eastern Orthodox and Episcopal churches have employed it for centuries. It does seem a bit out of place, however, for an evangelical church to adopt such a polity. Most denominations that fall under the umbrella of evangelicalism find either a presbyterian or a congregational governing structure the most suitable. The important thing to point out, however, is that even in episcopal polity, checks and balances are in place to hold clerics accountable. We encourage the WCG as it seeks to install these necessary checks and balances. This will enable members of the leadership to be directly accountable to one another and to an independently appointed board.

Pastorate and Tradition

As the WCG makes its way into the evangelical fold, the difficult question of "which fold?" must be raised. What are the implications? There are many. For example, in attempting to avert the danger of an unaccountable hierarchy, the WCG is turning its attention to evangelicalism in hope of finding a viable alternative. But here the WCG may encounter a problem. One of the current crises in Protestantism is the confusion of "the priesthood of all believers" with the office of the ministry. In the interests of emphasizing the equality of all believers before Christ, the pastoral office has come to be regarded as a mere function in the life of the church. At the time of the Reformation, Martin Luther did emphasize the doctrine of the priesthood of all believers, but he did not do so at the expense of diminishing the pastoral office. His point was that the pastoral office is to be distinguished from that of the laity, not in rank but in calling or "vocation."

In the present nonecclesiastical climate of our culture, there is little understanding of what the office of the ministry really is. It is hoped that the WCG will not "leap from the pan into the fire" in the coming years. In fact, it is our wish that all evangelical theologians give more serious consideration in future systematics to the doctrine of the church and the office of the ministry.

Evangelicals continue to experience an identity crisis, struggling to understand how the various denominations together constitute the church. While evangelicals fault the historic churches for turning liberal and forgetting what the gospel is, perhaps blame is to be equally leveled toward a movement that in many instances has maintained at least in practice, if not in principle, that the gospel can exist apart from the church.

Liberalism has indeed removed the gospel from the pulpits of many mainline traditions. And evangelicals have done a fairly good job of retaining some of the basic fundamentals of the faith. But they have done so at times by removing the gospel from the very environment that nurtures it and gives it life: the ministrations of the preaching and teaching office of the church. Without a clear understanding of this, the sacramental aspect of the gospel has been lost as well. This, however, is the subject of another book.

Here our point is as follows. As hundreds of denominations exist today, perhaps the lack of an understanding of the doctrine of the church is a large part of the problem. The autonomy and freedom which are part and parcel of the modern American identity do not necessarily coincide with the identity of the Christian as it is to be lived out in the context of the one, holy, catholic and apostolic church. Perhaps current evangelicalism has contributed as much to this problem as mainline traditions by helping to create conditions that are ideal for the proliferation of cults and adverse sects.

Shaped by Grace

The largest struggle the WCG will continue to face in the future will be the struggle the Christian church has always faced: the issue of free and justifying grace, or the proper distinction between law and gospel. Grace is not just a doctrine that is to be applied to isolated situations here and there. It must be part of the very life and fabric of the church and of the Christian. The gospel shapes the entire church and the Christian life. Whether one is talking about doctrine, polity, worship, stewardship, evangelism or vocations in life, it is easy to mix law and gospel to the point where the law and legalism become the constitutive shaping factor of the church rather than the gospel.

The law, in every instance, confronts humanity with the burden of *what we must do* and is quite capable of delivering guilt for our many failures. Thus the WCG under Armstrong was quite able to deliver condemnation and guilt, as is the case with all legalism wherever it is to be found. The gospel, on the other hand, tells us not what we must do but *what Christ has already done for us.* The law is couched in the imperative mood, while the gospel is in the indicative. The law commands while the gospel invites. The Christian does good works never "in order that" but always "because of." We do not perform good works in order that we might obtain right standing with God. We do good works because we are already in right standing with God in Christ.

The law-gospel distinction must also enter the theology of the WCG's statement of ethics. Legalism would impose on ministers standards beyond the parameters of Scripture. The WCG would do well to follow a general principle that is gospel-oriented: Where the Scripture is silent, there is freedom. A law-based approach—adopted far too often in churches throughout Christendom—would suggest that where the Scriptures are silent, human beings must speak, injecting human laws to fill in gray areas that the Bible does not directly address. Scripture knows no complicated codes beyond the simple, plain exhortations given to the church by its blessed prophets and apostles. It is through these that we come under the covenant of grace.

Concerning the ongoing struggles between those who have left and the current WCG, we hope the grace ministry to which the Lord has led them will enable all groups involved to work toward the good of the kingdom and continue helping the needy people who come to them. A parallel can perhaps be drawn with the situation in Russia, where the Lutheran Church Missouri Synod has been trying to plant a mission church; we have brought Russian pastors to our U.S. seminary for equipping to continue this work. Some ecclesiastical authorities do not like our presence in Russia, though, and have put up opposition. An American professor on our lecture team, Kurt Marquart, told us an old Chinese parable when we were considering this problem: Two teams of Chinese laborers were given the task of digging a tunnel through a hill. They decided to start at opposite sides of the hill, figuring that if they met halfway, they would have dug one tunnel twice as fast—and if they did not meet halfway or at all, in the end there would be two tunnels! We need to rejoice whenever, so to speak, there are groups digging into the work of the kingdom from different sides of the hill.

Paul had a sharp disagreement with Barnabas about whether to take Mark with them on a missionary journey (Acts 15:36-41), and the disagreement was so serious that the two friends could no longer work together. So they worked separately, and the work of the ministry went forward on two fronts instead of just one. Such is the mystery of the kingdom and the ways of God, who works in spite of us, and is there to grant grace, forgiveness and sound knowledge and doctrine—all of which are sorely needed in Christ's church today. That is why we are glad that the chief struggle for the WCG is the issue of grace.

We conclude by wishing the grace of God on a movement and a people that for many years were shackled by the heavy burdens of legalism. We celebrate the grace that has performed its marvelous work. Lives have been changed, sins have been forgiven, and destinies have been altered. And this, wonderful as it is, should come as no surprise, since God is in the business of making the impossible very possible.

Do this and live, the law commands,

It gives me neither feet nor hands.

A better word the Gospel brings,

It bids me fly, and gives me wings.[1]

Soli Deo gloria!

Appendix 1

Doctrinal Changes in the WCG Since 1986

The Doctrine of God

In February 1996 Tkach wrote: "Gone is our long-held view of God as a 'family' of multiple 'spirit beings' into which humans may be born, replaced by a biblically accurate view of one God who exists eternally in three Persons, the Father, the Son, and the Holy Spirit."[1] The WCG has published a very fine statement of faith concerning the doctrine of God:

> God, by the testimony of Scripture, is one divine Being in three eternal, co-essential, yet distinct Persons—Father, Son, and Holy Spirit. He is the one true God, eternal, immutable, omnipotent, omniscient, omnipresent. He is Creator of heaven and earth, Sustainer of the universe, and Source of human salvation. Though transcendent, God has a direct and personal relationship with human beings. God is love and infinite goodness.[2]

This statement is an accurate articulation of what Scripture and the ecumenical creeds confess concerning God the Father. This article captures both the transcendence and the immanence of God, a point which the non-Christian religions of the world do not believe, teach or confess. Evidently much of the theological reflection on this issue came as a result of what the WCG previously believed about Jesus and "the great gamble" theory, discussed briefly below.

The Doctrine of Jesus Christ

Previously the WCG taught that there was a possibility that Jesus could have sinned and that he could have failed in his humanity to understand numerous aspects of his own divine nature. This concept, which some have called the "great gamble" theory, was really the result of misunderstanding both the doctrine of the Trinity and the personal union of the two natures of Christ. Understanding the doctrine of the Trinity, however, also leads to a orthodox and traditional understanding of the person of Christ.

The WCG statement of faith now articulates that "Jesus is the Word. . . . As God manifest in the flesh for our salvation, He was begotten of the Holy Spirit and born of the virgin Mary, fully God and fully human, two natures in one Person."

It remains to be seen, however, whether the WCG will be able to fully realize the deep implications of the church's Chalcedonian Christology. In chapter three we offered a criticism of Armstrong's doctrine of Christ. The new confession the WCG has constructed to revise and correct Armstrong is a significant change.

The Holy Spirit

Where the WCG previously considered the Spirit to not even be God, it now confesses that the Holy Spirit, the "third Person of the Godhead, is the Comforter promised by Jesus Christ, sent from God to the Church." The statement of beliefs goes on to confess that the Holy Spirit is the "Source of inspiration and prophecy throughout the Scriptures, . . . the Provider of gifts for salvation and for the work of the gospel, and the Christian's constant Guide into all truth."

In June 1993 K. J. Stavrinides met with the church leaders and regional pastors along with Ambassador University staff in Pasadena to explain the doctrine of the Trinity. Joseph Tkach Sr. acknowledged at that meeting that as of December 1991 the doctrine of the Holy Spirit had been studied; the conclusion was that the Spirit is not an impersonal force as Armstrong had taught but rather a Person in the Godhead. In the December 1991 issue of *The Worldwide News,* Tkach noted, "We should all realize that this is an area that had never been carefully studied." The statement of faith includes and article called "The Law of Christ" which is in reality a restatement of the doctrine of sanctification, which is elaborated earlier. "Allegiance and obedience to our Savior" is said to come "through the Holy Spirit."

The New Birth

Armstrong taught that the common Protestant understanding of "born again" was heretical and would lead people away from cultivating godlike character in this life so they could become God in the next. In January of 1991 the WCG changed its position on this issue. We have already seen that the WCG no longer teaches that God is a family of two, the Father and Jesus Christ, but exists as a Trinity of Father, Son and Holy Spirit. Armstrong stressed that the God family would be enlarged as believers moved from being begotten to becoming born again. With the dismissal of the God-as-family teaching, there was no more need to understand the new birth as the way that the God family proliferates.

Anglo-Israelism

Changes in this doctrine came in 1992-1994. Lengthy study papers on this are available from the WCG. Through simple neglect, Anglo-Israelism seems to have faded into oblivion. It is no longer talked about or emphasized. However, the doctrine was, and perhaps still is in isolated cases, preached. In 1992 Joseph Tkach Jr. wrote to a minister exhorting him not to preach it: "All of our traditional proofs are based upon folklore, legend, myth, and superstition." On July 13, 1995, the following statement was published in Pasadena by the WCG administration:

> The Worldwide Church of God teaches that national identity and ethnic origin have absolutely nothing to do with the believer's standing before God. "There is neither Jew nor Greek, slave nor free, male or female, for you are all one in Christ Jesus" (Gal. 3:28). Certainly the knowledge of any biblical identity of modern nations does not forgive sin, assure salvation, or improve human relationships.

For over 50 years, the Worldwide Church of God taught that Great Britain and the United States of America descended from two of the lost ten tribes of Israel. However, while the Church has held certain beliefs concerning the identity of the lost ten tribes, it has never embraced all of the tenets of what is commonly called "British Israelism."

Today, after having carefully researched the tenets and history of its belief that the United States and Britain are the descendants of the ancient Israelite tribes of Manasseh and Ephraim, the Worldwide Church of God no longer teaches this doctrine. While it may be an interesting theory, there is simply a lack of credible evidence, either in the biblical account or the historical record, to support a conclusion regarding the modern identity of the lost ten tribes of Israel. We recognize that there were hermeneutical and historical inaccuracies in the Church's past understanding of this issue.

Therefore in accordance with the Church's historical position of a willingness to change when convicted that its teachings are biblically inaccurate, the Church no longer attempts to identify the modern-day descendants of the lost tribes of Israel. The Church has withdrawn from circulation all editions of its publication *The United States and Britain in Prophecy.*

The belief in Anglo-Israelism under Armstrong had been important due to the understanding of the role prophecy played. As is made clear above, the WCG no longer officially holds to Anglo-Israelism. We hope that all the ministers and members of the WCG will agree with this change and let go of the "old leaven" of Armstrongism. It is clearly unbiblical, racist and heretical.

Church Eras

By 1993 or so, the WCG had discarded the teaching that the church is in the "Philadelphian era" of Revelation 2—3. The WCG no longer believes that it is the only church to which this prophecy pertains.

The Sabbath

In January 1995 Joseph Tkach Sr. issued a "new covenant" document, in which he said: "There is nothing in the new covenant that says we are required to keep the Sabbath according to the rules of the old covenant." He went on, "Being Sabbath-keepers does not make us more righteous than other Christians." This document informed WCG members that at certain places the WCG had now officially departed from Armstrong's former teachings.

The 1995 *Statement of Beliefs of the Worldwide Church of God* reads concerning the sabbath:

> The weekly seventh-day Sabbath, which was enjoined upon Israel in the Ten Commandments, was a shadow that prefigured the true Reality to whom it pointed—our Lord and Savior Jesus Christ. Though physical Sabbath keeping is not required for Christians, it is the tradition and practice of the Worldwide Church of God to hold its weekly worship service on the seventh-day Sabbath (Saturday).

The WCG makes December 21, 1994, the official date on which this new attitude toward the sabbath began. Note the close proximity of this date to the publications and teachings of Earl Williams, who without a doubt played a significant role in bringing the grace teachings into WCG theological discourse. The issue of the sabbath and its application to grace and law became a clear point at which a discussion of grace could now be practically applied in an area that mattered dearly to members of the WCG.

Some have wondered about the WCG's current attitude concerning the Seventh-day Adventist doctrine of the sabbath. Tkach has acknowledged that the history of the WCG's understanding of this doctrine is as rooted in Seventh-day Adventism as was Armstrong, even though the latter, as we saw in chapter two, did not wish to acknowledge this fact. The WCG presently believes that its rejection of the sabbath under the new covenant is also a rejection of the sabbath as taught by Seventh-day Adventists.

Annual Festivals

The WCG has officially maintained that the observance of the sabbath is to be continued, but not as a doctrine binding on those who wish to omit it from their piety. The annual festivals continue to be observed in many WCG congregations. The statement of faith maintains that feasts will continue to be celebrated annually based on the feasts God gave to Israel in the Old Testament. The WCG now regards them as "memorials of

God's great acts of salvation in history and as annual celebrations of God's power, love, and saving grace in Jesus Christ" rather than what Armstrong maintained regarding the feasts up till his dying breath—that they were "ordained forever" to be observed in obedience to the command of the Lord.[3] The holy days that some congregations and members of the WCG continue to observe include the Feast of Tabernacles, Passover, the Feast of Unleavened Bread, Pentecost, Feast of Trumpets, the Day of Atonement and the Last Great Day (Lev 23:36).

Tithing

According to official WCG doctrine, triple tithing, prevalent during the Armstrong era, has been abandoned. The statement of faith maintains that "tithing is the Scriptural practice of giving a tenth of one's increase to God. Giving tithes and offerings was commanded under the old covenant, but is voluntary expression of worship and stewardship under the new covenant."

The Fate of the Unrepentant

It is maintained in the statement of faith that the fate of the unrepentant sinner is to "perish" in the lake of fire. "This death is eternal, and the Scriptures refer to it as the second death." On the surface this appears to still uphold the doctrine of annihilationism that Armstrong taught so adamantly. It is unclear whether the WCG has moved toward adopting the traditional teachings of Christianity, that the unrepentant will live on in continual torment in hades and the lake of fire (Rev 20:14-15) as the righteous live in bliss throughout all eternity in heaven. The authors therefore requested a second interview with Joseph Tkach Jr. On May 21, 1997, he stated that the WCG does allow some flexibility in this teaching and that some ministers do preach the doctrine of hell. He acknowledged that annihilationism is still embraced by many ministers as well as members. This answer concurs with the answer given in an interview conducted by *Cornerstone:*

> Do you still hold to "soul sleep," the concept of somebody not being conscious after death until Jesus' return, at which time they are raised?
>
> MF [Mike Feazell]: Yeah, that has always been the position of the Worldwide Church of God. It still is. But as fast as we say, "Well,

that's our official position," we also tell our members that it isn't the only way to interpret Scripture on this issue. These are things that we will not know for sure until we're all dead anyway. God knows what he's doing, and we probably wouldn't understand it if He explained it to us in clearer terms.[4]

One Hundred Years

Armstrong taught that there would be three resurrections: that of the faithful, who will rule with Christ during his millennial (one-thousand-year) reign on earth, that of the ignorant after the millennium, and the resurrection of sinners. Based on Isaiah 65:20, "for the child shall die a hundred years old," Armstrong contended that the period of time between the second and third resurrections would be one hundred years. This doctrine has been abandoned.

Nineteen-Year Cycles

Armstrong believed in drawing numerical parallels between periods of time in the early church and the WCG. He believed that nineteen years had lapsed between the Day of Pentecost and the penetration of Europe with the gospel in A.D. 50. Similarly, nineteen years separated the founding of the WCG (1934) and the broadcast of *The World Tomorrow* via Radio Luxembourg to Europe. Armstrong attempted to identify other such nineteen-year cycles. This doctrine has been completely abandoned.

Church Eras

Revelation 2—3 is no longer seen as necessarily depicting specific church eras corresponding to the churches in the text. The WCG now sees these two chapters and the message to the seven churches as a general exhortation to the whole Christian church at all times.

The Jewish Temple

The belief that the Jewish temple had to be rebuilt in Jerusalem before the return of Christ and that the old covenant sacrifices would be reinstituted has also been abandoned. It should be stated as an aside that modern fundamentalist dispensationalists would do well to follow the good example of the WCG here.

The Roman Catholic Church

Armstrong had vehemently taught that the Roman Catholic Church was the "Great Harlot" of Revelation. The WCG now recognizes that Roman Catholics are part of the body of Christ if they trust Christ as Lord and Savior.

Openness

The former closed-door policy has been abandoned. The headquarters and any other properties and churches of the WCG are open for all to visit.

Pentecost

This feast is still celebrated as a memorial of the giving of the Holy Spirit and the beginning of the church.

Divorce and Remarriage

The WCG still teaches that the marriage union between husband and wife is sanctified and blessed by God. Although God hates divorce, the WCG now allows for legal divorce in the case where fraud, adultery, sexual promiscuity, abuse or abandonment takes place.

Marriage Between Believers and Unbelievers

This is still discouraged in the WCG, as it is in most evangelical and Protestant churches; Roman Catholics similarly encourage marriage within the church.

First Tithe

This is no longer seen as obligatory under the New Covenant. Members are exhorted to see the first tithe as a regular standard to strive toward, just as members of many denominations within the Christian fold are encouraged to tithe.

Second Tithe

This tithe is no longer required or obligatory.

Third Tithe

Also no longer obligatory. Needy members are assisted out of church funds and general offerings. This varies, of course, in different congregations throughout the WCG.

Race
There is no racism or segregation advocated in WCG doctrine. Interracial marriages are not forbidden.

Women
Women are regarded as equal partners of God's grace. Women are encouraged to participate in all levels of ministry, with the exception of the office of pastor, a calling that is still reserved strictly for males.

Clothing and Personal Appearance
Laws regarding dress codes, hairstyles and the like were among the earliest to be abandoned following Armstrong's death. Personal discretion and gospel freedom are now advocated, much to the applause and approval of many members.

Faith, Healing and Medicine
In the spring of 1987 the WCG changed its teaching and practice by allowing members to seek medical attention when needed. In 1988 Bernie Schnippert and Joseph Tkach Sr. authored a revision of the booklet *The Plain Truth About Healing* which delineates these changes. The WCG believes that God still heals, albeit as he chooses.

Makeup
In the November 14, 1988, issue of *The Worldwide News,* Joseph Tkach Sr. wrote: "The Bible does not give us plain statements forbidding the use of cosmetics." It had previously been forbidden for women to wear makeup, as this was regarded as defiance toward God, one's husband and the church.

Interracial Marriage
This was previously considered a sin, given the implications of Anglo-Israelism. The July 30, 1990, issue of *The Worldwide News* mentions that in some societies people are tolerant of such marriages. Today interracial marriages are not believed to bring reproach upon Christ.

Appendix 2
Interview 1

On January 28, 1997, George Mather traveled to Pasadena and met with the three top leaders in the WCG: Pastor General Joseph Tkach Jr., whose present titles also include being president of Plain Truth Ministries and chairman of the board of the WCG; Gregory Albrecht, editor in chief of *The Plain Truth* magazine for five years, whose employment with the WCG goes back to 1969; and Mike Feazell, former director of church administration and now executive assistant to the pastor general. Feazell has been a member of the WCG since the early 1970s and said to us that his job "is to oversee the superintendent of ministers and mission." The following is a transcription of George's conversation with Tkach, Albrecht and Feazell.

GM: *What role did Mr. Tkach Sr. seem to play regarding the doctrinal changes and the eventual entrance of the WCG into the evangelical Christian community? What role did your father play in that?*

JT: Shortly before the death of Herbert Armstrong, he had mentioned to my dad some items that were on his mind that he felt needed to be better explained.

GM: *This is Mr. Armstrong?*

JT: Yes, and he wasn't specific, but maybe was specific on one item or two, but generally that there were some things that he should look into and explain them better. . . . I think my dad's contribution was that he had the courage to, let's say, stand up and orchestrate the explanations of the flawed teachings we had had for so many years. And while he did not articulate it himself, it would have never happened if he hadn't authorized that it be done and that people be assigned to have seminars and get together with our leadership in our denomination and review our former teaching and show what was biblically correct. So I think his role was having the courage to stand up and say, "This must be done," and assigning us to do it.

GM: *And what was the response of the leadership in the church when that request was made known?*

JT: Mixed reviews. A very quick polarization occurred, because you had people on one side who were devotees of Herbert W. Armstrong's teachings and on the other side you had those who had already been praying and studying, hoping that God would answer their request for some reform. So it wasn't really a lot of neutral, middle ground.

GM: *Mike Feazell, how did it affect you when you found out that Mr. Tkach was requesting a reevaluation of some of the teachings?*

MF: Well, as Joe was saying, it was not so much that he was requesting a reevaluation of teachings as it was a mutual recognition by Joe, his dad, and me that there were certain issues that needed to be addressed. In other words, it was kind of a mutual coming to those kinds of things you find because you work very closely together all the time. The doctrines of Herbert W. Armstrong were being challenged by letters that came in here, and we had to answer those letters, and after his death we were no longer able to rely on Herbert Armstrong's explanation. At that point we realized he was dead, and we took more care researching our answers to make sure that we were answering things in a consistent way. We began to find inconsistencies in Herbert Armstrong's reasoning and his answers on certain issues. And it wasn't a question of everything all being changed at one time with "let's go and review all of our doctrines." It happened one at a time over a period of time, kinda like one domino led to another. So there wasn't any point at which we said, "Let's just reevaluate all our doctrines." It was just a matter that we wanted to be honest with Scripture, and so anytime something came up that looked like a challenge to our teaching, we were willing to look at it. But we didn't set out to line up doctrines and check them out. It happened one doctrine at a time.

I think that for me, the determining factor to a large degree was that Herbert Armstrong was dead, and so we had a different mindset. There wasn't the mindset of, well, God will show Herbert Armstrong if there's a mistake in our doctrine that we had before, because he was God's man and so on. Instead, it was the responsibility that now fell on Joe's dad, and he wanted to be honest with Scripture, and we wanted to support him in that and make sure the answers were consistent and that Herbert Armstrong wasn't in the picture. We started from the premise that Herbert Armstrong had been right, but then in honesty we found out that he wasn't, and we had to deal with each issue as it came up.

GM: *Did you do this inquiry collectively, or was sort of a private investigation going on where you all started to see inconsistencies and difficulties and you ended up collaborating? How did that develop?*

MF: It was a little different on each issue. You know, it's like a snowball. The first thing that changed was somewhat insignificant to us, like a crack in a dam. . . . We realized Herbert Armstrong could be wrong, but we always knew that Herbert Armstrong could be wrong anyway. So we didn't worry about it very much.

GM: *How so? You just said that you knew him to be wrong.*

MF: Well, he's a human being, so we knew any human is going to have his mistakes and so we try to just say—for me it was like this. I saw that he was wrong and my conclusion was "Well, God allows, you know, for us to be human and make mistakes." But of course Herbert Armstrong wouldn't be wrong in any major thing. Only in these interpretations of details, so after six years or so of seeing the snowball getting bigger and bigger and bigger, we finally had to realize it was far more than just insignificant details, of God just allowing him to make this mistake and that but he is really the Elijah to come and the endtime prophet and all that kind of thing. We eventually came to see, but that took a period of time.

GM: *What were some of the teachings in question?*

MF: The very first teaching in question was insignificant. It was Herbert Armstrong's presentation of the night Israel went out of Egypt. He believed that the Israelites killed the lambs and then went out of Egypt the following night. He believed that there was a day in the middle in which they spoiled the Egyptians, and in his [Armstrong's] typical advertising style, he wrote that in very strong capital letters and in condemnatory terms [warned] anybody who would believe otherwise. . . . Well, a few of our ministers came forward and said, "Look, you know Mr. Armstrong is dead now, and we brought this up a couple of times, but it never really went anywhere, but we feel compelled to bring up the fact that he makes a big deal out of this particular point, and we believe he is wrong."

GM: *Talk to me about your attitude toward members going to different churches, to churches of different denominations.*

MF: There is nothing wrong with attending another Christian church where you are going to make a contribution or where you are going to be nurtured. At the same time I think it is important for any Christian to know, as one writer put it, there are two reasons to stay in a church. One reason is that you need what that church offers. Another reason is that church needs what you can offer. Should I stay or should I go? And evaluate what your motives are. Look for God's will.

I must be honest with you, I don't feel we need a great campaign to say that you need to stay in our church and you better stay here, or here is why you need to stay here, or our church is better for this reason and for that reason. . . . It is better to be going to the church down the road and be nurtured than sitting home, or than . . . coming to our church and feel like they are dying on the vine. They need to be nurtured. And if Pastor Jones can nurture them better than me, I want them down at Pastor Jones's church.

GM: *Would you have talked this way six years ago, Mike?*

MF: Six years ago, yes.

GM: *Seven years ago?*

MF: Seven years ago, maybe. Eight years ago, no!

GM: *Your relationship with Jesus Christ and the way you understand the importance of the gospel to people, the way you are talking about now, the priority is to make sure that they are at the right church*

*and not sitting at home, but I think that seven or eight years ago you
would have said, "No, you have to be here [a member of the WCG],
otherwise you are going the way of apostate Christendom." How has
this reform affected your emotions, your feelings, and how may it have
affected your family members? Can you respond to that?*

MF: Well, anytime you have friends who decide to reject you as a
person or reject something very important to you as a person, and go to
something else . . . then that's painful and hurtful. So yes, there have been
friendships where that has happened, where people now view me as . . .

GM: *That has happened with family members?*

MF: In my family, not really. In my wife's family there have been
a few family members where that has been the case.

GM: *Getting back to Mr. Armstrong again, did he understand the
gospel? What did he understand the gospel to be?*

MF: Armstrong took the words of the gospel of the kingdom of God
and he believed that the gospel should therefore be about that. OK, so
far so good. But then he took the words "the kingdom of God" and he
attached the Herbert W. Armstrong interpretation of what the kingdom
of God is about. To Herbert Armstrong, the kingdom of God had to do
with the establishment of the government of God over all the nations
at the return of Christ. . . . In his premillennial eyes, he saw a thousand
literal years of Jesus reigning with the saints over the physical nations
of the earth. . . . A thousand years before the introduction of the new
heavens and the earth. To him, when Christ arrives on earth at the
Second Coming and establishes this government over the nations and
brings about a thousand years of utopian peace, that's the definition of
the kingdom of God. So for Herbert W. Armstrong, the gospel was the
gospel about the arrival of Jesus on earth at his Second Coming to
establish the kingdom of God on earth.

GM: *Not now, but later?*

MF: Not now, but later. He saw it as a future event to be declared
and announced now. So if you said to Herbert Armstrong, "OK, yes,
but what about the life and death and resurrection of Jesus, or what
about justification and salvation?" he would say that's part of the
gospel, but it's not the focus. The focus is on the Second Coming of
Christ and the establishment of the kingdom, because it's the gospel

of the kingdom of God. It's as though other verses that spoke of the gospel of God or the gospel concerning his Son, and there are many, didn't occur in the Bible. . . . He [Armstrong] said that in the first and second century the gospel was changed by the followers of Christ from a gospel that Jesus himself preached to a gospel about the person of Christ. That was his rhetoric. So Jesus came proclaiming a gospel about the kingdom of God interpreted the way he saw it. Then the church was established, and before long apostasy set in. In the second century, the curtain comes down, and what emerges after the second century is a different church, a church that proclaims a different message, a different gospel, about the person of Christ, not the message that Jesus himself brought. . . . Armstrong would say, "No one preaches the true gospel that Jesus himself preached. No one preaches that today." That's what he meant when he said that no one preached the gospel for nineteen hundred years. He meant no one has preached this Second Coming, the literal establishment of the kingdom and government of God. That's what he is talking about. He doesn't mean no one has preached the life, death and resurrection of Jesus. So, does he know what the gospel is? Does he know what salvation is? Yes, but he's got his emphasis in the advertising rhetoric, screwing the whole thing up.

GM: *How did that affect you?*

MF: How did it affect me? I grew up with this focus on the gospel. I knew I had repented of my sins, and I believed in the death and resurrection of Jesus for my salvation and so on, but my focus as far as gospel—to me gospel meant this future thing. Well, when I began to study the Scriptures carefully, [I] learned that no, the gospel is wrapped up in the person of Jesus Christ first of all, and whatever Armstrong said all this time is not true. That's not an obscure gospel. That's not a misinterpretation. That's what the Scriptures say the gospel is. And yes, that includes the Second Coming, but it's kind of the other way around. There is a second coming. I don't buy all this premillennial stuff personally myself. I see a new heaven and earth. That's all peripheral. I don't care about that. What I care about is what the Scripture says the gospel is. So this is what has to be proclaimed . . .

GM: *What is the gospel according to your understanding right now?*

MF: We go to 1 Corinthians 15, and it's exactly what Paul said the gospel is. And that Joe and I have talked about many times. Joe speaks about it in the same kinds of terms, that it's like the example of Peter, where Peter knows Christ, he spends three and a half years with him. He's with him all the time. He's under his teaching, he has a relationship with him. What kind of a relationship is it? It's a good relationship because it is with Jesus. But when the chips are down, he's denying Christ. However, after the resurrection and after Pentecost and the Holy Spirit comes, he isn't talking about things like "Is the kingdom going to be set up now?" or "When are you going to declare yourself to the Jews? When are you going to declare you're the Messiah?" Jesus said, "Don't even talk about it. You don't even know what the Messiah is all about. You know me, we have a relationship, but you don't know what's going on. You don't have a clue. You just wait." After Pentecost now, he [Peter] is preaching the Gospel. Well, for me, I grew up praying regularly, you know. I studied the Scriptures. I believed God. I had a relationship with God. We did not preach praying to Jesus. That was sort of foreign to us. I have now come to have a personal relationship with Jesus.

GM: *Describe this relationship.*

MF: It was like Peter's.

GM: *Mr. Tkach, I would like to ask you the same question I asked Mike.*

JT: Two things I would add to what Mike said. If you were to ask me ten years ago the classic question that D. James Kennedy asks in *Evangelism Explosion*—you're standing before Jesus and he says, "Why should I let you into my kingdom?" how would you answer?—I would have been one of those who said, "Because I have been striving to be the best man I can be." That's how I would have answered ten years ago. Of course now I would give a totally different answer, because it's Christ's righteousness imputed to me. So I have grown in my understanding.

And on the practical side, looking at Peter as an example before and after Christ's crucifixion and resurrection, Peter was living for himself. He had a relationship with Jesus. It was a great relationship with Jesus. But sometimes I get the impression I was too busy trying to qualify for the kingdom of God. Now I live for Jesus.

GM: *What has the cost been for you now that you live for Jesus? In terms of the effect of these changes on family members, friends, what has the cost been, if any?*

JT: Boy, I can put it in a couple of different categories. Emotionally, it's impossible even to describe. But I have people I grew up with, people at the high school, college, who won't talk to me, ranging from won't talk to me to thinking I'm demon possessed. We have an incredible loss in our corporate structure, loss of income, loss of membership, death threats that seem to be unrelenting.

GM: *Even today?*

JT: In fact just three weeks ago, after church services, one of the members of the Global Church of God, who happened to come and visit, tapped me on the shoulder and told me that if he had the authority he would kill me. That got people's attention standing around us. All I could tell him was that I was sorry he felt that way and I didn't feel that way toward him. He said he would do just like they did in ancient times—"I would cut your head off." So you get that kind of stuff.

GM: *I'm sitting here kind of shocked. . . . Did you lose family members?*

JT: I have two sisters, both married with children. My younger sister and her husband have remained with our fellowship. My other sister and her husband have left and went with the United group. They are leaders in their hierarchy. And through it all we have been able to maintain our family relationships. But it's difficult.

GM: *But you have had death threats, even three weeks ago at your church, where someone would say they would, if given the authority, execute you as they did in the Old Testament by cutting your head off. You have lost family members for the sake of the gospel. If your sisters were here now, what would you say to them?*

JT: That I love them and pray for them, and I think at some point in time—well, one is doing fine. The other one with the United group? Boy, what would I say? I love them and I pray they will come to see all the things God, in his mercy, has helped us to see.

GM: *Greg?*

GA: I probably would have answered that question, George, in terms of when Herbert Armstrong died in 1986, he was the glue that held our movement together. . . . There was so much that didn't make sense, but Herbert Armstrong had to say, "This is the way it is. It's going to be this way because I say so." Shortly thereafter I began, for a variety of reasons, to reevaluate my life, and that includes my life as a Christian and my life as a minister. I came to the conclusion in the late eighties that my life in the Worldwide Church of God had consisted of being in control, or being in authority, or being under authority. And so my life as a parent was primarily being in charge of my kids. And my life as a husband was being in charge of my wife. And my life as a college administrator was being in charge of students. My life as a minister was being in charge of members.

I began to notice that Jesus didn't talk a lot about being in charge and controlling people. In fact, it was quite the opposite that Jesus called you to. It was giving up and surrendering, and it was a very different kind of life altogether. And so with Philip Yancey, who wrote *The Jesus I Never Knew,* my experience would be that I came to know Jesus, someone I had known about but never had known personally in the way that when you open your heart up to him, and when you believe in him, and when you accept him as Lord. And it's an entirely different kind of relationship, and it comes through—as many of our members have gone through—deep, dark agony, soul searching. What about this and what about everything I have believed in, and what about Herbert Armstrong, and what about my minister, and what about my church, and what about the things I gave up? Etc., etc., etc. I believe that many of our members have come to that kind of conclusion through all of this. It's a wonderful conclusion, but it's a journey through the valley of the shadow of death.

GM: *What has been the cost in terms of relationships with family and friends?*

GA: I would say about the same as Mike and Joe. I have lost many, many friends who either do not understand what has happened in my life, do not agree or think I've become—curiously, though I've been a minister for many years, they think I've become a religious nut. They think I've become born again.

There has been an interesting theme throughout the Worldwide Church of God. When we have talked about Herbert Armstrong before,

Mike pointed out in his rather long sound byte—it's important to talk about this—Herbert Armstrong is a very complex person. It's very difficult to talk about Herbert Armstrong without a lot of rhetoric, and he was not consistent. One of the things in the Worldwide Church of God that we seemed never to really want to do was to be a church. We wanted to be a college. We wanted to be a foundation. We wanted to play with the gospel. But we never wanted to be a church. And so when you talked about really being a church, and really being a Christian, and really being a minister, and telling people on airplanes, you know, "What do you do?" [they ask], "I'm a ah, ah, college admin . . ." you know, as opposed to "I'm a minister of Jesus Christ." People in our church said, "Whoa, you mean you tell people you are a minister of Jesus Christ?" Well, yes. Well, what do they say? Well, they say, "That's interesting," or, you know, we start talking about the Bible or whatever. We have a curious kind of culture in that we were kind of ashamed of being Christians in some respects. Probably there was this deep belief down, you know, a lot of our beliefs were assailable, eminently so, and we didn't want to get into having to argue about why we believed x, y and z with people.

But in any case, the fact that you come out of the closet and say you're a Christian and a minister—this is somewhat new to people. You actually start reading and studying the great Christians down through time. You start listening to Christian radio and reading Christian literature. It's a big, big change to your friends. They say, "What are you doing that for?" "Well, because I'm a Christian." So there has been quite a misunderstanding of people, most of whom have left with our splinter groups or gone nowhere over our religious awakening. They say, "Well, you guys are just like kids in a candy store. You're just reading about this guy and reading about the other guy." Well, of course we are. You know, that's what Christians do. Christians want to read about Martin Luther.

GM: I will ask all of you the same question. *How do you understand the nature of the church? What do you think the church is? What is its substance? What makes the church the church? Have you worked through that issue yet?*

GA: The church is, of course, both visible and invisible, isn't it? And I like what [a certain person—unnamed] says about that; he says that sometimes people think of the church as a group of people that are somehow established together in some corporate structure. Some people like to think of it that way. Some people like to think of the church as all of God's people in the world who are doing his work wherever they are, and you don't know who they are. They are invisible to you. . . . The church is wherever God is doing His will and wherever Jesus rules in the hearts of men and women. I don't lie awake at night worrying where that is.

GM: *Let's say you walk into a church: how would you know that is the church?*

GA: There are two things in the New Testament that we hear. One is that we have love one for the other, in John, and secondly, . . . whether or not the Holy Spirit is leading us. Neither of these lend themselves to an immediate judgment as to the Christianity of the individual that you are looking at.

GM: *You would have, for example, many religious and fraternal groups for that matter where you would find love for each other. It's not the church. Many might claim the Holy Spirit is guiding them, but it's not verifiable. What else would you look for?*

GA: I would look for the historic and essential Christian faith. The doctrines espoused by the major creeds early in the history of the church. I believe believers need to embrace those. They may not completely comprehend them, but I believe the believers gathered together, if you're looking for an organization, need to embrace those.

GM: *What has been the response of the Christian community, both positive and negative?*

GA: For the most part, the response has been positive.

JT: The people that early on came alongside us to extend to us the hand of fellowship, so to speak, and stand with us and encourage us would be the following: some of the faculty of Azusa Pacific University, faculty like Les Blank, dean of the Graduate School of Theology, Earl Grant, professor of world religions, and other faculty members there. Those are two that we got to know the best. They were very supportive and saw early on how difficult and complex this struggle was. Ruth Tucker from Trinity Evangelical—she's a church historian, she teaches church history. Some individual pastors like Bill Brafford, who pastors the El Monte Four

Square Gospel congregation, who introduced us to their denominational leader, President Dr. John Holland, and people like George Mather,
who pastors at Sherman Oaks Lutheran Church and introduced us to their
denominational leader, Al Barry.

A personal comment! I found it fascinating, looking at the Christian
community, that someone who is very charismatic like the Four Square
Gospel on the one hand and then someone—I'll use the term "tradi-
tional-conservative," historic Christian faith, Lutheran—who was very
different, but those were the two groups, very different, but the first
two groups to come alongside us. We met with the leadership of the
Lutheran Church Missouri Synod in St. Louis, and some of the
theology professors at Concordia University like Drs. Chuck Manske,
Robert Dargatz, Rod Rosenbladt and some others. They were very
gracious and encouraging and supported us through our changes. Then
there was Hank Hanegraaff of the Christian Research Institute,
founded by the late Dr. Walter Martin.

Another [thing] I wanted to mention, because we noticed that there
was such skepticism in the Christian community as a whole, and especially from the counter-cult ministries, that this was a genuine article and
that the Holy Spirit was really moving—what we need to do is look at all
the people who have ever written about the WCG, and let's go to them
and tell them, "Look, some of the things you have written in the past are
true, and some is untrue, and we have changed. So a lot of what's contained
in those books is not factual and no longer true." In looking through
authors of books like that over the years, *Kingdom of the Cults* was sort
of an magnum opus work, and at that time Hank Hanegraaff had succeeded Dr. Martin. So let's go to someone like that who has written one
of the magnum opus works on our church and tell them the whole story,
and one at a time, we started addressing counter-cult ministries, the
authors of books, and that's how we met you. Others who were helpful
were Dr. D. James Kennedy and Don Mazat, an LCMS Lutheran who
does a program on Jubilee Network. D. James Kennedy, Hank and Don
Mazat did radio interviews with us and were the first ones who really got
the word out in the street that this was a real change.

GM: *[Concerning the Lutheran interview], were you talking about the
interview you gave while meeting with the LCMS leadership in St. Louis?*

JT: Yes.

GM: *What were some of the negative responses from the Christian community as you tried to come into and be a part of the historic Christian church?*

JT: Among the counter-cult ministries, one in particular [which will remain unnamed] was probably the most difficult group. . . . They were constantly second-guessing our changes and always trying to "scoop" like a major newspaper approach, trying to get the scoop and present this inside information, and rarely talking with us; they appeared to be trying to get sensationalism. The net effect was this. [This cult-watch organization's] inside scoop approach and implying that we were being duplicitous and dishonest was to undermine our credibility with our own people, so that we couldn't present the most effective information to get them across the bridge from heresy to orthodoxy.

GM: *Did it hurt you in any way that you know of other than just the remarks? Were there consequences?*

JT: I would get letters from people who would tell us, "You're not telling us the whole story, and I read this from the [name of cult-watch organization]," and so they would leave and join one of the aberrant splinter groups. Now they are unreachable. They got it from the inside source, from the [name of cult-watch organization]. Now dynamite won't blow it from their minds. What was sad was that for the most part, they would write these things with little or no contact with us. And the few times they did make contact, it was just a one-sided, one-dimensional conversation . . .

For example, here is a lady who has embraced all of the changes and has a relationship with Jesus, and she's wonderfully happy. Her husband didn't embrace any of the changes and is in fact part of one of these splinter groups and is an ex-Marine, and he's following his wife all through the house when they are at home, reading from the aberrant literature to her—our old stuff from the past. Reading it, following her around the house, reading it in her face, trying to get her to recant because she has embraced the changes. So this guy goes to [unnamed cult-watch organization] and tells them his wife is thinking of leaving him and she's going to break up the marriage because of these changes. [The cult-watch group] seems to have taken his side over hers until we pointed out that as an ex-marine, he's a bit on the abusive side with his wife, and he's following her around reading this stuff in her face. They didn't seem to have a clue as to the reality of that.

Another instance is that they would report that we were being heavy-handed or abusive in the way we treat some of our ministers, and they would cite Bob Collins as one of our ex-pastors who left and is free of all of this. Bob Collins left thinking that he was one of the two witnesses and is as aberrant as they come. So they would give a false report, and it just didn't help as a whole.

Since that time I don't think I have had any contact with any of them except for once or twice, a letter exchange. I think Greg has talked with them on the phone, and I think some apologies might have been exchanged, and I'm happy for that. I appreciate their zeal and the mission they feel they have, but boy, it was sure a zeal without wisdom, without knowledge.

GM: *That's the problem with a lot of the cult ministries. They are well-meaning Christians who really aren't prepared properly to deal with the nature of this kind of ministry . . .*

JT: There was another counter-cult ministry up in Canada, and she and her husband are ex-Jehovah Witnesses. As an aside, we have noticed that whatever background they have, it becomes the lens through which they view, and it colors their approach, and I don't think they even realize, but it's because they have established themselves as a counter-cult ministry and they have a following. . . . They finally wrote us a list of twenty-five questions. We wrote back answers to all the questions. We wrote back answers to all the questions, because all the answers would be required for them to sanction us as being orthodox, and they were not ready to do that. They wanted to come and meet with us, which was great. So we ended up spending a couple or three hours with them answering the same questions in person that were asked in the letter.

GM: *What is her background? Does she have any theological training?*

JT: I do not think so. I'm fairly certain she does not. As an ex-Jehovah's Witness, she was one of the ones with missionary fervor. . . . So we went over the same questions, but this time orally, and after every question we gave an answer and she would say, "Well, if that's true, that's great." And the next question, "Well, if that's the way you really feel, that's good." And after hearing that several times as a qualifier, I finally said, "You know, I am getting the feeling you don't believe our answers." And she said, "Well, you guys have a doctrine of justified lying." We don't even know what that is.

GM: *It's a heavenly deception doctrine.*

JT: We were too self-righteous to ever do anything like that. So when we explained that we don't [practice justified lying] and that we are telling her what we really believe, and there is no justified lying, there was an incredible change in her. She did begin to get excited and happy and started treating us fairly warmly after that, but . . .

GM: *It is true that with some cults, to believe the ultimate good, one may lie.*

JT: That's what she learned from her Jehovah's Witnesses.

MF: If that's true, how does she know we're not lying about our doctrine?

GM: *Obviously there is nothing to [gain] by doing what you have done other than loss of membership and money. I don't think this has been a great pleasure for all of you.*

GA: Another individual, Janis Hutchinson, who wrote a book, *Out of the Cults and into the Church,* she was a Mormon. In fact, she had an incredible story about being kidnapped by the Mormons, held against her will, starvation diet, an incredible story! We talked with her, and she was absolutely thrilled with what was happening with the church. But she had known a number of members of the church who had written to her for advice, etc., etc. We invited her to some of our ministerial conferences, so she saw the process. She saw the transition. She saw how we were trying to teach our ministry about where we have been and where we are going. But she couldn't. She wanted us to handle everything overnight, and again, lacking training, [she insisted that] we are going to have to. We need a strategy. We need tactics, and we just don't do this overnight. So essentially, we sort of parted ways. She saw some examples within our fellowship who were impatient themselves . . .

MF: She wanted us to violate the principles that were written down in her own book. In her own book it says specifically, "You can't vilify the cult leader because there is an emotional bond the people need to get past." She said that you can't vilify the traditions of the church or of the cult because, there again, there is an emotional bond with good times and so on. But she wanted us to trash Herbert Armstrong, and she wanted us to tell our members that we will not, and we must not any longer, keep any of the Old Testament festivals. Well, that's . . . the very reason that we were originally determined to not make those mistakes . . . because of the advice in her book. And yet she's turning around and giving us the example of a double standard.

GA: A good example of what you said, a lovely woman, a peach of a lady, in over her head because she didn't have the theology and the history of the whole thing, just her own experience of coming out of Mormonism and being with a lot of Mormons.

JT: [Another unnamed ministry in Canada] didn't really affect us much here in the U.S., but it was a problem in Canada. Whereas Janet Hutchinson and [unnamed cult watch group] created problems for us [here].

GM: *I have a couple more questions to ask. How many congregations do you presently have in the United States?*

MF: In the United States, 425. There are 530 worldwide.

GM: *How many before the reform?*

MF: About the same.

JT: What has happened is that in one congregation, a third left and two-thirds stayed. In another congregation, two-thirds left and one-third remained . . .

GM: *So the congregation remains, but the people have left. The size is smaller . . .*

MF: There is some fluidity in the number of congregations with us all the time because we use rented halls. So sometimes it's more convenient for more members to change to another place, and so sometimes that changes things . . .

GM: *How many pastors do you have?*

MF: Currently we have 230 full-time pastors in the United States, I think. Most of them have dual parishes. We are moving away from that in a deliberate manner, but it will take us awhile. Worldwide, we have about 450 pastors.

GM: *Tell me about downscaling of staff and expenses.*

JT: One time we had one thousand employees at the Pasadena property. That's when we had the college in operation here and we were doing all the media work with television and radio. Now we have 160 employees in Pasadena. So that's just a little over 10 percent remaining.

GM: *So you have about 10 percent of the original staff?*

JT: Yes.

GM: *I understand that the property here in Pasadena is up for sale?*

JT: Yes, we have a broker, and we signed a contract with him in February of last year. It has taken them from February to December [1996] to complete their due diligence preliminary title search of each property. It's a complex property. There are fifty-one acres, seventy-two buildings on it. . . . And because of the complexity of the property, it does not lend itself to the three traditional ways of appraisal. So, our broker said, they prefer not to put a price on it. Let them market it. The property's value would definitely be higher than replacement costs. At least that's what we have been told.

Our property is right on the route of the Rose Bowl Parade. It borders Orange Grove Boulevard, which is where the parade begins, on the corner of Del Mar and Orange Grove Boulevard, and then it turns on Colorado Boulevard and goes five miles up Colorado Boulevard. Our property borders Orange Grove and Green, which is the next street.

GM: *What about your facilities in Texas?*

JT: We have about twenty-four hundred acres in Big Sandy, Texas, which is one hundred miles east of Dallas. We had a campus there since the 1950s, and the property consists of about three hundred acres of college facilities, dormitories, classrooms, cafeteria, auditorium. It could handle about one thousand to twelve hundred students. The educational program consists of no accreditation until around 1990, when we merged the campuses. We now have approval from several accreditation associations.

GM: *What do they offer in degrees?*

JT: Twelve different majors, computer science, etc., and the degrees offered were A.A., B.A. and B.S. We were accredited by SACS. Our facility in England was closed in 1974. The value at Big Sandy is being appraised in the next three months by Deloitte and Touche, which is one of the big six accounting firms, as well as the most highly regarded real estate consultant in the nation. Both facilities will be closed unless someone does comes along and buy it before the semester ends.

GM: *What will you do regarding the training of ministers?*

JT: We will eventually partner with other Christian universities and award scholarships there after we establish a Christian endowment fund . . . with the proceeds from the sale of our properties.

GM: *After your properties are sold, you will be relocated?*

JT: We will relocate here somewhere in southern California, probably stay close to here because we have built such a nice network of fellowship and brotherhood here with Azusa Pacific, Fuller Seminary, Christian Research Institute, Four Square Gospel, Concordia University, Irvine. Does it make any sense to move to Dallas, Texas, and start all over again and go through all our past history?

GM: *Are you experiencing any growth in membership now that the reform has toned down a little bit?*

JT: We haven't yet gone out and tried planting any new churches because we are still in the phases of rebuilding the infrastructure. We did our first training of lay pastors a few weeks ago and gave certificates to thirty new lay pastors. Two of those were really excited about planting new churches. In the U.S. we are baptizing about one hundred people a month. Internationally, we have had some real interesting things develop. Probably the most noteworthy would be in Angola, which has been a country that has been torn apart by civil war. Nobody has been able to go in there, and we have thirteen thousand members there now and talking with another eight thousand people, and recently ordaining forty-five ministers there.

GM: *How long was your training program for ministers?*

JT: Well, the lay pastors' training was two weeks long. And we had a nice mix of presenters for that from Azusa Pacific, Fuller and some of our own people.

MF: These are people who have worked in one form or another in a local church. These are not pastors but helpers . . .

GM: *How will you develop your theology? Will you create a systematic theology or be more eclectic?*

JT: Probably so. I don't know, since there are maybe fifty systematic theologies out there. I don't think we have to re-create the wheel.

GM: *Let me put it this way. What if one of your churches wanted to baptize children. How would you handle that?*

JT: We already have some who have baptized youth. . . . With infants, so far that has not come up as an issue yet.

GM: *But at some point you will have to have some kind of a structure to your theology. You can't leave it totally open-ended, right?*

MF: We're not convinced you can't leave it totally open.

GM: *Really, then if someone wanted to baptize an infant, that may be allowed?*

MF: Yes.

JT: We are moving from it was forbidden to baptize anyone under eighteen to we are having people getting baptized eleven or twelve years old now.

MF: In doing that, we would want to give guidance though, to somebody who did do that, about how those Christian churches that have history and tradition in that practice. In other words, they need to know what they are doing . . .

GM: *Are you creating your own material for teaching your people?*

MF: Yes.

GM: *If someone wants to be a member of your church, they don't just come in and say, "Can I join?" There is some sort of formal training they go through?*

MF: We are in our early, early stages of being able to do anything. We are creating in-service training programs for our pastors who are currently in their jobs by putting on taped programs from Christian universities of first-class [caliber]. We just recently had a Christian administration leadership [seminar] led by Alister McGrath. We used tapes of his class from Regent College, and then we developed a little curriculum to go with that. And we will be giving two classes a year to all ministers who are employed along these lines on a continuing basis. Then in terms of doctrine and policy and so on, we just need to build that as we go.

But our general approach is that peripherals need to remain peripherals; thus we are giving much liberty to those areas. But we do not want those to be done haphazardly and foolishly. We want them to be done with people knowing what they are doing. So our approach is to explain what the accepted Christian positions are, then take the position that in our fellowship you can hold any of these positions. But we do ask that people do not get divisive. We do leave room for different interpretations.

Appendix 3

Interview 2

What follows here is the responses of Joseph Tkach Jr., Mike Feazell and Greg Albrecht to questions posed by George Mather in a second interview conducted in May 1997. We include most of the interview.

1. Will the time come when the WCG will openly renounce Herbert W. Armstrong?

When we discuss our opinion of HWA with ministers and members, we are open and honest. We have openly repudiated and apologized for much of Herbert Armstrong's teachings, including those he considered core issues. We have openly denied his belief that God called him to have modern-day ministry similar to the ministries of Ezekiel, Elijah and other Old Testament prophets.

We have openly and totally transformed the publication *The Plain Truth* from a narrow sectarian publication filled with prophetic speculations and overarching emphasis on the legalism to one that focuses on the gospel of Jesus Christ.

Many former members consider such admissions and changes as an ipso facto open renunciation of Herbert W. Armstrong. That is one reason why many have left us. That is in part why our income is down and why we have suffered so much pain these last few years.

We see no reason, however, to renounce everything that Herbert Armstrong ever said or did. Remember: he insisted that the Bible was the final authority in matters of faith, doctrine and ethics. Believing this has made our reformation easier. Furthermore, Herbert Armstrong had always taught that Jesus had died for our sins. Our baptismal formula read, "Because you have accepted Jesus Christ as your personal Savior, soon coming King, and high priest in heaven, we baptize you not in any sect or denomination of men, but into the name of the Father, the Son, and the Holy Spirit."

So while we lament the many mistakes Herbert Armstrong made and renounce those things he taught contrary to Scripture, we see no reason to tar and feather him and burn him at the stake. We believe that it is far more gracious and Christian to point out his errors than to place ourselves in the role of his final judge.

Further, *renounce* means to give up something, to reject or disown something. We can reject particular teachings of HWA, as we already have, but we cannot reject or deny the fact that he founded the WCG.

2. Does the WCG view Armstrong as heretical?

The term *heretical* means different things to different people, and we therefore prefer not to use it. To some it means non-Christian. To others it means erroneous teaching. We openly admit that many of HWA's teachings were erroneous. Almost every Christian leader has had some erroneous teachings. HWA had many, and some were heretical. But we do not judge *him* to be a non-Christian. We accept his own testimony that he accepted Jesus Christ as his own Lord and Savior. We also have seen and experienced that he and the WCG were instrumental in leading many people to accept Jesus Christ as their personal Lord and Savior.

While the church believes that much of what Herbert Armstrong taught was heretical, we see no biblically based necessity or pastoral benefit for our fellowship in making this kind of corporate judgment about the man. Members are free to come to their own conclusions.

3. Did Herbert W. Armstrong preach the gospel in the narrow sense of the word?

We will give some excerpts below, but we will also comment on them in advance to give some perspective. All of HWA's writings contained some errors. Some people focused on the errors and became fixated on prophecy or lawkeeping. Others, by the grace of God, were able to focus on the truth of salvation by grace through faith in Jesus Christ.

Often his presentation of the gospel was a mixed bag. Generally, he understood the gospel as the kingdom of God, which he believed to be the family of God, with special emphasis on the millennial rule of Jesus and the saints. This was the message that he said that Jesus brought. This gospel, he said, had been suppressed. He believed in its place that all other churches had substituted a message about the person of Jesus. Therefore churches had substituted a message about the person of Jesus. Therefore the primary focus that Herbert Armstrong placed in his preaching was not on Jesus Christ and him crucified, but on what he considered God's kingdom—the future reign of the glorified Jesus.

Yet every year at Passover time, the church kept the Lord's Supper in memory of Jesus' crucifixion. That he died for our sins was the central message of this service.

In Herbert Armstrong's *Autobiography* he related his own conversion. He focused on Acts 2:38: "Repent and be baptized every one of you in the name of Jesus Christ for the remission of sins, and you shall receive the gift of the Holy Spirit" (p. 319 in 1986 edition). After being baptized, Herbert Armstrong said he knew "that the terrible heavy load of sin had been taken off my shoulders. Christ paid the penalty for me. All past sins were blotted out by His blood. My conscience was clean and clear" (p. 320). Furthermore, perhaps his most repeated radio broadcasts were a series on the book of Hebrews. In this series he continually stressed how Jesus ascended into heaven, where he now serves as our living high priest, making intercession for us.

Everyone who was ever baptized in the WCG answered yes to this question in the baptismal ceremony that HWA wrote: "Do you accept Jesus Christ as your personal Savior?"

Part of the reason some people focused on salvation through Christ is that HWA emphasized the authority of the Bible. He wanted every member to read the Bible by themselves and to believe it. By pointing people to Scripture, he helped some people put their faith in Jesus Christ.

HWA was convinced that Christians should obey their Savior, and he was correct about this. Faith does lead to obedience. However, HWA had a major misunderstanding as to *which* biblical laws Christians ought to obey. Moreover, his writings often implied that people who didn't keep the right laws weren't really saved. He meant that lawkeeping was a consequence of faith, not a cause of salvation, but nevertheless, many people concluded from this that HWA taught salvation by works. Even though HWA knew that salvation was by grace, not by works, he found it difficult to make his position clear.[1]

4. Certain books written by Herbert W. Armstrong contained heretical statements. They were edited and reprinted after Armstrong's death. How and why did this occur? Please explain.

Even before HWA's death, his books and articles were edited before they were reprinted. In some cases he made the edits himself, and in other cases he approved edits made by others. Often the edits were stylistic. Sometimes they were doctrinal. When articles and booklets were reprinted, HWA did not knowingly perpetuate errors. When he believed his previous understanding to be in error, he edited the text, just as any author would when it came time to reprint.

After HWA died, this process continued at a faster pace. Since HWA was a full-time employee of the church and writing was part of his job, and since the church paid for all of his publication costs, his writings fall into the legal category of "work done for hire." The copyright was held by the church, not by HWA, and therefore the church could continue to edit his works as we saw the need.

After Herbert W. Armstrong died and his booklets came up for reprinting, they were reviewed to see if edits were necessary. If we saw statements that were erroneous or unlikely, we would delete them. This was the only sensible course of action. There is no point in publishing things we know to be in error. But we could edit only according to what we understood, and we did not understand at first the magnitude of HWA's errors. Initially we saw a great deal of truth in HWA's booklets and felt that they *should* be reprinted as a service to our readers, if we just took out the errors. We certainly had no thought of giving the misimpression that Herbert Armstrong's teachings were all without error.

As time went on and we learned more, and as our inventory of booklets was depleted and we needed to reprint, we realized that it was better to simply cancel the reprinting of his booklets.

5. Will the WCG develop an accountability structure within its church polity in order to assure the Christian community that theological changes will remain orthodox?

We are not aware of any polity structure that could accomplish this. Unorthodox teachings have occurred in other denominations, whether they are congregationally governed or more hierarchical in governance. Structures cannot ensure orthodoxy. The Christian community itself is not immune from theological error.

We are fallible, and therefore we must allow for some doctrinal change. We would *like* to have a mechanism to guarantee that changes can only be for the better, but we are not aware of any such accountability structure.

However, the WCG has joined the National Association of Evangelicals, and our membership (rather than a polity structure) gives the Christian community some assurance that the WCG intends to continue to accept the seven points found in the NAE statement of faith. As long as we remain members of the NAE, we give the Christian community some assurance of orthodoxy.

Our *financial* accountability is shown in an annual audit by Cooper and Lybrand. We are also *legally* accountable in the almost one hundred nations we are incorporated in. The president/pastor general of the WCG, as an officer of the legal entity of those nations, could be subpoenaed in any of those nations. Few Christian leaders have that level of legal accountability! Nevertheless, at the president's own request the bylaws are being revised to make him accountable to the church board, and that the board members not be appointed by the president. There are a few other bylaw changes that are being discussed with attorneys, and it is hoped that all such changes will be completed within the next couple of years.

We are also improving our *ethical* accountability structures. With input from our pastors, we are developing a ministerial code of ethics, which all ministers, including the president, will have to sign.

6. If the church governmental structure remains in its present form, how will the WCG preserve the theological changes that place them in the historic faith? It appears that another pastor general could return to the former teaching of Herbert Armstrong unless accountability with checks and balances is established.

As noted above, we do not know of any church governmental structure that could guarantee that changes could only be for the better. We do agree that some checks and balances are appropriate, but we have not yet finalized all of them and are in consultation with attorneys.

While some may think it is theoretically possible for the church to return to its former teachings, that is really not feasible. Such a concern does not appreciate the depth of the changes in the hearts of people. With every passing day, fewer and fewer wish to go back to our former teachings. Most of our membership rejoices in the freedom Jesus has brought them.

One check and balance is already functioning even though it is not required in our polity. The current pastor general does not take sole responsibility for setting church doctrine. The positions described in our *Statement of Beliefs* and in these answers are based on discussion and consensus among senior ministers and church officials.

A *powerful* check and balance is already in place: members are free to leave the denomination. Most members do not believe in all of HWA's doctrines, and if some future pastor general attempted to go backward, we believe that a huge exodus would occur. Such a reversal would, organizationally speaking, be catastrophic.

Because of the concern that we not go back, we have started an in-service education program that is training our entire United States pastorate in the historic Christian faith. This program is the model for several of our international areas. Our biblical interpretation class includes a twenty-four-tape program produced by Regent College featuring Gordon Fee and Bruce Waltke.

For those church pastors who can afford it, we encourage them to attend accredited theologically orthodox schools or seminaries. Already we have ministers that either attend or are enrolled in distance learning programs at Regent, Fuller, Trinity Divinity, Bethel, Covenant, Liberty, Azusa Pacific and others. Their education will help us maintain the orthodox Christian faith in our midst.

In many communities our ministers have joined ministerial associations. Some have begun to be trained by the Billy Graham organization. Others participate in Promise Keepers. Many attend worship seminars and other types of conferences put on by a variety of Christian leaders.

7. If a new governmental structure with accountability is to be established, when do you plan to do so? Please give a time frame.

As also noted above, we plan to amend our bylaws, and this will include a bylaw enabling the board to remove the pastor general for unethical behavior. We believe that all such changes will be complete in five years.

8. What is the WCG's position on the Reverend Earl Williams? What role, if any, did he play in the WCG reform?

Earl Williams played a role no greater or smaller than any of the several pastors who were enthusiastic in embracing and teaching to their congregations the published doctrinal reforms. Earl also wrote a couple of articles for church publications that were supportive of the reforms. However, after his initial positive support of the church's changes, Earl decided to lead a part of his congregation in a split from the WCG. His actions created spiritual division, forcing the WCG to terminate his membership and revoke his ministerial credentials.

9. What is the WCG's present position on the doctrine of eternal punishment (hell)?

While we believe in eternal punishment (Mt 25:46), commonly known as hell, we believe that God has given us to understand in only a limited way the nature of life in the age to come, and we do not wish to be dogmatic on the specific details of hell. We do teach that the suffering of eternal punishment will be beyond any punishment suffered in this world and that the reality of it will be much worse than the symbols. And these symbols also teach us more about God's nature. For example, the lake of fire and brimstone is not a place of cruelty but a place of God's perfect justice.

Most evangelical Christians believe that the wicked will remain in conscious torment forever, but some evangelical Christians believe that they will *not* remain conscious forever.

For example, Michael Green in *Evangelism Through the Local Church* (pp. 69-70) writes: "To be sure, the New Testament is emphatic about the possibility of eternal ruin. To be sure, it speaks about hell in a direct manner. But it does not teach conscious unending torment of those who are eternally separated from God. The language of 'destruction' is the most common description of final loss in the Bible."

The NAE does not have an official position on this question, and neither do we. The WCG used to teach in a dogmatic way that the wicked will be annihilated, and we taught this doctrine in a way that promoted division in the Christian community. We repent of using the nature of eternal punishment as a litmus test of truth, and we ask forgiveness for the damage we have done to the unity that Christianity ought to have.

10. Has there been an intentional attempt to hang on to existing members of the WCG by not making further changes (e.g., memorializing Herbert W. Armstrong, not changing the church's constitution)?

No.

We are more often accused of bashing HWA than of memorializing him. If one were to ask our members, we doubt few would say that we have stopped making changes. Change is a part of our church culture. Some believe we are making changes too fast, while others believe it is too slow. Our track record over the past decade shows us repeatedly willing to make doctrinal changes that we knew in advance would cause some members to leave. Our primary concern is faithfulness to Jesus Christ and Scripture, not hanging on to members.

However, we do not want to drive members away, either. As servants of Jesus Christ, we want to teach and help our members, and we cannot do this if we alienate them with unnecessary changes, changes that are not required by Scripture.

We find it somewhat humorous that any would think that we would try to hang on to members by refusing to change the church's bylaws. As far as we know, our members have *no* emotional attachment to our bylaws. It was only with the last two years that members even knew what was in them. And we have explained that we are consulting with attorneys to make changes.

11. Christian churches and related parachurch organizations make

financial information available to the public. Will you mind providing
that information for us (e.g., salaries of staff, expenses)?

Each month we publish the amount that has been donated and how
much has been spent. We have also reported the percentage of money
that is used for our many congregations and the major departments in
Pasadena. We do not publish how much specific individuals give, nor
do we publish how much specific individuals are paid.

Some Christian organizations publish individual salaries, and some
do not. If we were to make that information available, we would
publish it for our members before we disclose it to outside researchers.

Unlike most denominations, we rarely collect offerings in our
worship services. Instead our members mail their contributions to our
headquarters, which then distributes the funds where they see the
needs. Some congregations are learning that they are receiving more
from denominational headquarters than they are giving. And the re-
verse is also true. Accountability is thus a two-way street. We comply
with all financial reporting requirements of the law. We publish our
annual financial report in *The Worldwide News*. We openly discuss the
details of our denominational budget with our pastors.

12. What are your present beliefs about eschatology?

We believe that Jesus Christ is King of kings and Lord of lords. With
his birth, the kingdom of God was established in a new and direct way
among human beings. God has given him all authority in heaven and
earth. With his ascension, he reigns at the right and of the Father. The
converted have been born again and have entered the kingdom of God.
They have eternal life and will receive immortality. We look forward
to Jesus' personal return and his judgment of the living and the dead,
and the fullness of the kingdom in the new heavens and new earth. All
who believe in him as Savior will be given immortality and will live
with God forever; those who do not believe will be condemned to
eternal punishment.

We used to have dogmatic views on many additional aspects of
prophecy, and we criticized those who held other views. Today we
recognize that equally sincere believers can come to different conclusions as to what Scripture teaches on some of these issues.

For example, in the earliest centuries of Christianity, most Christians believed that Christ would reign for one thousand years after his return. This was a premillennial view. But eventually the amillennial view came to be dominant for many centuries. Today many evangelical Christians believe the amillennial view, and many believe the premillennial view. Some believe that the Scriptures teach a postmillennial view.

We do not question the conversion, intelligence or faithfulness of people who hold these views. Rather, we recognize that the different conclusions are based on different approaches to interpreting the inspired writings. Some tend to view predictions literally; others tend to view them figuratively. Both hermeneutical approaches can be illustrated from the New Testament use of Old Testament prophecies. We also recognize that apocalyptic literature plays a large role in the debate, and that apocalyptic is notoriously difficult to interpret.

Our position is that millennial views are *adiaphora,* indifferent matters on which Christians can hold different opinions. No particular view is needed for salvation, and no particular view is necessary for the church to perform the functions God has assigned it. What is important is that Jesus Christ will return in power and glory, judge all people and reward the saints, and they will rule forever. No matter what happens, all the saints will be wonderfully happy, and no one will be gloating about getting the interpretation correct.

We have already commented on individual eschatology, specifically whether the wicked will be forever conscious of their punishment. The important part of the doctrine is that the wicked will be punished in perfect justice.

One further aspect of eschatology: the destiny of those who never heard the gospel preached in this age. We believe God makes righteous provision for those who never heard the gospel and that he is perfectly fair and does not show favoritism. God wants *everyone* to come to a knowledge of the truth and to an opportunity for repentance (1 Tim 2:3-4; 2 Pet 3:9). Exactly how he does this is open to speculation. On the other hand, we reject the concept of universal salvation.

13. Pastor General Joseph Tkach has been known to say that the governmental structure of the WCG is episcopal. In light of the fact that all Christian church bodies holding to an episcopal form of government, including Rome, have boards established to assure ac-

countability of leadership, does the WCG have such checks and balances now? Please explain the following:

a. If yes, what are the checks and balances already existing?

b. If no, will a board(s) be established through the voting of church members or pastors, or be appointed by the pastor general?

c. If the structure is to remain the same as in the past, why?

a. The leaders of the church are accountable to federal and state laws governing church organizations. We view our accountability to Jesus as of paramount importance. We do not view ourselves as free to do as we please. We are and continue to move toward greater accountability toward our members and the greater Christian community as a whole. For additional comments on checks and balances, see the answer to question 6.

b. Our governmental structure already includes a board, whose members are appointed by the pastor general. As previously mentioned, we are in discussion with attorneys to revise the bylaws. Nevertheless, our general structure fits into the category of episcopal, although it is not exactly the same as any other church. However, it should be noted that formal structures cannot ensure that leaders remain morally or theologically correct. History shows that entire denominations can go astray no matter what kind of boards and accountability structures they have.

We understand why people would seek some assurance that the WCG remain orthodox and accountable. Thousands of people have been hurt by the doctrines of the traditional, hierarchical WCG as led by Herbert Armstrong, and they would like assurance that no more people will be hurt. But unfortunately, there is no legal structure that could guarantee that. Even churches with congregational government can become abusive and even heretical. Nevertheless, we trust in God that the planned changes in the bylaws will provide as much assurance and safety as possible.

c. As mentioned above, our bylaws will be amended, one of which is to make it possible for the board to expel the pastor general. The structure will change; however, we wish to complete our consultation with attorneys before we make any further disclosures.

14. Please explain the WCG understanding of ecclesiology.

This is a broad subject, and we are not sure what your specific interest is. Let us briefly comment on a few areas.

The church is composed of all who have faith in Christ. This is the invisible church. Christ also calls on believers to meet together. This is the visible church. There is only one invisible church; there are many visible churches, as different believers gather in different locations at different times. We regret the fact that these visible churches do not always reflect the unity that they should. Indeed, we admit that the traditional WCG led by Herbert Armstrong took a divisive approach. We repent of that, ask for forgiveness and seek to work with other Christian denominations and churches as we serve Christ in similar ways.

The church's oneness is in Jesus Christ. The church is the body of Christ, called to continue the work of Christ in the world. The functions of the church include worship, preaching the gospel, equipping the saints for works of ministry, and works of mutual love toward neighbors. God distributes spiritual gifts to the members of the body, and he wants them to work together, each according to his or her particular gift(s). Pastors exist to facilitate this cooperation among the members.

The church's holiness is the imputed righteousness of Christ. The church's catholicity comes from the fact that the church membership is not limited by time, geography and ethnicity. The church's apostleship comes from its embrace of the eternal gospel proclaimed by Jesus and his disciples.

The church is an imperfect organism composed of sinners dependent on the grace of God. Though the church is to be separate from the ways of the world, it is not to depart from the world. Jesus' commission to take the gospel to the world, making disciples of all nations, requires that the church enter the world. The church is not to live in isolated communities, but rather, it is to bring its loving, gracious Christian witness into all cultures and for all peoples.

In the visible church there are tares along with the wheat. Pastoring such a mixed body requires wisdom, grace and love. Christians in the visible church should strive to maintain each congregation as a spiritual healing community. Where this is happening, people will experience God's love.

Scripture does not mandate any particular governmental structure for the church. In some theological categorizations the sacraments are considered part of ecclesiology. See question 16 for a discussion of them.

15. Does the WCG accept the Apostles', Nicene and Chalcedonian creeds?

Yes, even though the creeds do not have a specific role in the WCG liturgy. Our foundation and reference point is Scripture. We accept the creeds only because we believe that they synthesize certain teachings of Scripture and the witness of the Spirit in the historical church. But when there is a question as to what the creeds mean, we look to Scripture as ultimate authority.

16. How does the WCG understand the sacraments? Are they ordinances, symbols or means of grace?

We understand them as commanded symbols. Jesus commanded his apostles to baptize those who repent and believe, and to teach subsequent disciples to do likewise. But we do not believe that the water itself washes away sins. A person is justified (which means that all sins are forgiven) by faith, not by performance of a ritual. The baptism is a symbol, not only of washing but also of burial and resurrection. We baptize by immersion those who repent and believe the gospel.

We understand the bread and wine of the Lord's Supper to be symbols too. When Jesus instituted the bread and wine as commemorative of his death, he stood before the disciples and said, "This is my body, which is broken for you." But when he spoke those words, his real body was right there, and it was not yet broken. We believe that he was speaking figuratively, not literally. Similarly, when he said the cup was the new covenant in his blood, he was speaking figuratively. Yet we realize that merely viewing them as symbolic is likewise too limiting. We recognize that in some sense God's grace is present and experienced by the believer. However, we do not accept the Roman Catholic [or Lutheran] view that the sacraments themselves convey grace.

Notes

Chapter 1: Forgive Us Our Trespasses

[1]Joseph Tkach Jr.'s "Forgive Us Our Trespasses" was reprinted in the July 15, 1996, edition of *Christianity Today.*

[2]We have recorded one instance of a cult becoming orthodox. Larry Nichols and George Mather, *Dictionary of Cults, Sects, Religions and the Occult* (Grand Rapids, Mich.: Zondervan, 1993), includes an article on the Holy Order of MANS, which has become Eastern Orthodox.

[3]David Covington, ed., *Crossroads: Life After the Worldwide Church of God* (1996; available from P.O Box 70012, Nashville, TN), p. 1.

[4]The number of members, pastors, churches and so on is a question we posed in interview 1. The figures reported are estimates. See appendix one.

Chapter 2: How It All Began

[1]Herbert W. Armstrong, *Mystery of the Ages* (Pasadena: Worldwide Church of God, 1985), p. 20; emphasis ours.

[2]Herbert W. Armstrong, "The Autobiography of Herbert W. Armstrong," *The Plain Truth*, September 1957, p. 21.

[3]Armstrong, *Mystery of the Ages*, p. 11.

[4]Herbert W. Armstrong, *Autobiography of Herbert W. Armstrong*, 2 vols. (Pasadena: Worldwide Church of God, 1986), 1:55.

[5]Armstrong's autobiography is balanced by several other good sources. Among the better ones are Joseph Hopkins, *The Armstrong Empire* (Grand Rapids, Mich.: Eerdmans, 1974), and Paul Benware, *Ambassadors of Armstrongism* (Nutley, N.J.: Presbyterian & Reformed, 1975). Numerous other sources are listed in the bibliography.

Armstrong's *Autobiography* underwent eight editions: 1957, 1958, 1959, 1960, 1967, 1973, 1974 and 1986. Unless otherwise indicated by date in our notes, we quote from the final or 1986 edition.

[6]Chapter 5 of volume 1 of Armstrong's *Autobiography* is dedicated to Armstrong's belief that he was the originator of public opinion polls. He titles this chapter "Pioneering in Public Opinion Polls."

[7]Ibid., 1:120.

[8]Ibid., 1:187.

[9]Ibid., 1:243.

[10]Marion McNair, *Armstrongism: Religion or Rip-Off?* (Orlando, Fla.: Pacific Charters, 1977), p. 91.

[11]Armstrong, *Mystery of the Ages*, p. 14.

[12]Ibid., p. 16.

[13]Armstrong, *Autobiography,* 1:293-94.

[14]Ibid., 1:297.

[15]Ibid., 1:300.

[16]Armstrong, "Autobiography," p. 9.

[17]Armstrong, *Autobiography,* 1:369.

[18]Benware, *Ambassadors of Armstrongism,* pp. 23-24.

[19]J. H. Allen's *Judah's Scepter and Joseph's Birthright,* 16th ed. (1917). Allen's book was well known at the time for advocating Anglo-Israelism. We include here several instances where Armstrong is relying on Allen. Allen wrote in his sixteenth edition of *Judah's Sceptre and Joseph's Birthright:* "But the great bulk of Israelites are not the Jews, just as the great bulk of Americans are not Californians, and yet all Californians are Americans" (p. 71). Armstrong's 1967 edition of *The United States and British Commonwealth in Prophecy* states: "Jews are Israelites just as Californians are Americans. But most Israelites are not Jews, just as most Americans are not Californians" (p. 82). Allen writes: "The name Jew is derived from, or rather is a corruption of, the name of Judah. . . . Hence it is that the names Jew and Jews are applied *only* to the people who composed the kingdom of Judah" (p. 67). Armstrong writes: "Remember that the term 'Jew' is merely a nickname for 'Judah.' Hence it applies to the one nation, or house of Judah ONLY" (p. 80).

Joseph Tkach Jr. acknowledged that Armstrong was not the originator of Anglo-Israelism: "From an ethical point of view: It is a well known fact that Mr. Armstrong did not originate this teaching. In fact earlier editions of *The US and BC in Prophecy* plagiarized vast portions of a book entitled *Judah's Sceptre and Joseph's Birthright.* It is not possible to say that this was revealed to Mr. Armstrong, when in fact, we can see where he copied it from—including the historical errors" (letter from Tkach to Mike Swagerty titled "Israel in End-Time Prophecy").

We have in our possession further evidence of Armstrong's plagiarizing. This includes several letters, one from the Canadian British Israelism Association stating as much and one from attorney William Reynard stating that the Ambassador publication "Has Time Been Lost?" was "next to an exact copy" of another work, therefore rendering the copyright of the Ambassador publication invalid.

[20]Armstrong, *Autobiography,* 2:47.

[21]Ibid., 2:147.

[22]Armstrong explains in detail all that transpired in the founding of the colleges. See especially ibid., 2:139-326. Also, Joseph Hopkins does an outstanding job in *The Armstrong Empire* of ferreting out of Armstrong's *Autobiography* the significant details in the story of Ambassador College. The reader should refer to pages 42 and following to refer to the story of Ambassador's beginnings.

[23]McNair, *Armstrongism: Religion or Rip-Off?* pp. 93-94.

[24]Ibid., p. 95.

[25]Ibid., p. 100.

[26]Ibid.

[27]Walter R. Martin, *Martin Speaks Out on Cults* (Ventura, Calif.: Vision House, 1983), p. 128.

[28]These included the Associated Churches of God, the Twentieth Century Church of God, the Church of God—the Eternal, and the Foundation for Biblical Research, a 1978 offshoot of the latter called World Insight International, and the Universal Church of God formed in 1981.

The Associated Churches set an early precedent for a current issue in the WCG by rejecting a theocratic church government in favor of a congregational polity. For more information on each of these groups, the reader should consult the recent edition of J. Gordon Melton's *Encyclopedia of American Religions* (Detroit: Gale, 1996). Melton provides details on names of founders, membership and publications of each of these groups.

[29]These incidents are well documented in major newspapers which covered the suit. Also, sources listed in the bibliography dating after 1978 also contain much more detail about the proceedings than we can give space to here.

[30]Armstrong, *Autobiography,* 2:584-85.

[31]As recorded by Russell Chandler, "Herbert W. Armstrong to Divorce Second Wife," *Los Angeles Times,* April 22, 1982, sec. R, p. 16.

[32]Jack Kessler, open letter of fourteen pages to the Board of Directors of the WCG and the Council of Elders, December 30, 1981, p. 2.

[33]J. Gordon Melton, *Encyclopedic Handbook of Cults in America* (New York: Garland, 1986), p. 102.

[34]Examples include an Associated Press article, "Church, State Appear to Be on Collision Course in California," *St. Petersburg Times,* November 3, 1979; and Stephen Bolettieri, "Trouble in Two Heavenly Paradises Continues," *Los Angeles Herald Examiner,* January 15, 1983.

Chapter 3: Anatomy of a Cult

[1]Alan Gomes, *Unmasking the Cults* (Grand Rapids, Mich.: Zondervan, 1994), p. 7.

[2]Ibid., p. 8. An appendix to Larry Nichols and George Mather, *Encyclopedic Dictionary of Cults, Sects, Religions and the Occult* (Grand Rapids, Mich.: Zondervan, 1993), provides a breakdown of the different religious families and the various sects and cults that emerged from the parent religions.

[3]Although a number of Herbert W. Armstrong's earlier works will be amply cited, the authors rely heavily on his last book, *Mystery of the Ages* (Pasadena, Calif.: Worldwide Church of God), published in 1985, just prior to his death—so that it serves as a "last will and testament" of sorts. It is an important source because it articulates what Armstrong believed and taught right up to the end, despite the fact that the WCG was about to undergo drastic changes under Armstrong's handpicked successor, Joseph Tkach Sr.

[4]Armstrong, *Mystery of the Ages,* p. 45.

[5]Ibid., p. 42.

[6]Ibid.

[7]Alan W. Gomes, "The Worldwide Church of God: Acknowledging the 'Plain Truth' About the Trinity?" *Christian Research Journal,* Spring/Summer 1994, p. 30. Gomes quotes from Armstrong's essay "Why Christ Died—and *Rose Again!*" *The Plain Truth,* April 1963, pp. 9-10.

[8]Armstrong, "Why Christ Died," p. 10.

[9]Sometimes this view is called "patripassionism" from the Latin *patri* (God) + *passion* (suffers), or literally "God suffering."

[10]Mather and Nichols, *Dictionary of Cults, Sects,* p. 322.

[11]Herbert W. Armstrong, *Just What Do You Mean, Born Again?* (Pasadena, Calif.: Worldwide Church of God, 1962), p. 11.

[12]Armstrong, *Mystery of the Ages,* p. 47. Armstrong also used John 7:37-39 and Acts 10:45 to teach that the Holy Spirit is poured out.

[13]Armstrong, *Just What Do You Mean, Born Again?* p. 13.

[14]Ibid., p. 86.

[15]Ibid.

[16]Garner Ted Armstrong also contributed to the WCG's teachings on the doctrine of the immortality of the soul in his *Do You Have an Immortal Soul?* (Pasadena, Calif.: Worldwide Church of God, 1957).

[17]Armstrong, *Mystery of the Ages,* p. 87.

[18]Herbert W. Armstrong, *Why Were You Born?* (Pasadena, Calif.: Worldwide Church of God, 1957), p. 26.

[19]Armstrong, *Just What Do You Mean, Born Again?* p. 40.

[20]Herbert W. Armstrong, *Is There a Real Hellfire?* (Pasadena, Calif.: Worldwide Church of God, 1974), p. 15.

[21]This has been the majority opinion throughout church history, but at various times there have also been otherwise orthodox Christians who have held an annihilationist position. If this were the only point at which Armstrong deviated from traditional views, he would not generally be considered unorthodox. But given his views on the other major doctrines considered in this chapter, he is clearly placed outside orthodoxy.

[22]Alan Gomes has written a good summary of the doctrine of annihilationism in "Evangelicals and the Annihilation of Hell, Part 1," *Christian Research Journal,* Spring 1991, pp. 14-15.

[23]Armstrong, *Mystery of the Ages,* p. 234.

[24]Galatianism is explored more deeply in chapter five.

[25]Mather and Nichols, *Dictionary of Cults, Sects,* p. 324.

[26]Herbert W. Armstrong, *The United States and Britain in Prophecy* (Pasadena, Calif.: Worldwide Church of God, 1954), p. 47.

[27]Walter Martin's book *The Kingdom of the Cults* (Minneapolis: Bethany House, 1985), pp. 310-17, gives an in-depth treatment of Anglo-Israelism in general and Baron's arguments specifically. Baron is referred to in Martin's book as "one of the greatest Hebrew scholars of the Christian church."

[28]See Armstrong, *Mystery of the Ages,* pp. 149-50.

[29]Ibid., pp. 24-25.

[30]Elements of this view of the seven churches are associated with dispensational theology and certainly were not original with Armstrong. Dispensationalism had its origins in the nineteenth century, chiefly in England, and then spread in America among numerous conservative Protestant movements and churches.

Chapter 4: A Modern-Day Reformation?

[1]Joseph Tkach Jr., "Forgive Us our Trespasses," *The Plain Truth,* March/April 1994.

[2]Ted Johnston, "Our Legacy in the Worldwide Church of God," *The Worldwide News,* January 21, 1997, p. 4.

[3]Ibid., p. xiii.

[4]Ruth Tucker, "From the Fringe to the Fold," *Christianity Today,* July 15, 1996, p. 30.

[5]Joseph Tkach, "God restored These 18 Truths: How Thankful Are You for Them?" *The Worldwide News,* June 1986, p. 1.

[6]David Neff, "The Road to Orthodoxy," *Christianity Today,* October 2, 1995.

[7]A letter to the authors by William Meyer dated June 20, 1997.

[8]This account were given in our third interview on June 17, 1997, at the WCG headquarters in Pasadena.

[9]Earl Williams, "Homes," *The Plain Truth,* January 1994, pp. 8-11.

[10]Earl Williams, "Which Church Is God's True Church?" *The Worldwide News,* June 14, 1994, p. 2.

[11]Jon Trott, "The Saga of a Cult Gone Good," *Cornerstone* 26, no. 3 (1977): 42.

[12]Philip Arnn, "Tkach Clarifies 'Sabbath' and 'True Church' Doctrines," *Watchman Expositor* 12, no. 1 (1995): 20.

Chapter 5: Reactions

[1]Philip Arnn, "Tkach Clarifies 'Sabbath' and 'True Church' Doctrines," *Watchman Expositor* 12, no. 1 (1995): 2.

[2]Ibid., pp. 3-4.

[3]The Lutheran Church Missouri Synod, with its confessional theology, emphasis on the sacraments and the means of grace, and use of the historic liturgy, does not really fit in this section titled "Evangelicals." But in other ways, such as the preaching of the gospel, the movements overlap.

[4]Ruth Tucker, "From the Fringe to the Fold," *Christianity Today,* July 15, 1996, p. 32.

[5]"New Beginning, New Leadership for the Worldwide Church of God," *Christian Research Newsletter* 9, no. 1 (Winter/Spring 1996): 13.

[6]Tucker, "From the Fringe to the Fold," p. 32.

Chapter 6: From the Outside Looking In

[1]Author unknown; this poem was recited to me (Larry) by Dr. Wesley Smith in his outstanding lecture on Galatians when I was a student of his in college.

Appendix 1: Doctrinal Changes in the WCG Since 1986

[1]Joseph Tkach Jr., "Personal," *The Plain Truth,* February 1996, p. 1.

[2]*Statement of Beliefs of the Worldwide Church of God* (Pasadena, Calif.: Worldwide Church of God, 1993, 1995), p. 2.

[3]Herbert W. Armstrong, *Mystery of the Ages* (Pasadena: Worldwide Church of God, 1985), p. 167.

[4]Jon Trott, "The Saga of a Cult Gone Good," *Cornerstone* 26, no. 3 (1997): 43.

Appendix 3: Interview 2

[1]In the response Joseph Tkach sent to us, he quotes liberally from Armstrong's writings. We are not going to reprint those excerpts here. The references are from

various works of Armstrong, including *What Do You Mean . . . Salvation?* and booklets *A World Held Captive, Millions Do Not Know What Christ Really Was! What Do You Mean . . . The Unpardonable Sin?* and finally *God's Holy Days—or Pagan Holidays—Which?* In all of these quotes Tkach, Feazell and Albrecht maintain that Armstrong professed essentially that Jesus died for the sins of the world. They also admit that Armstrong had difficulty articulating a clear doctrine of grace and salvation apart from works.

Bibliography

Selected Writings of Herbert W. Armstrong

Armstrong, Herbert W. *Autobiography of Herbert W. Armstrong.* 2 vols. Pasadena, Calif.: Worldwide Church of God, 1986.

──────. *Do You Have an Immortal Soul?* Pasadena, Calif.: Worldwide Church of God, 1957.

──────. *Is There a Real Hellfire?* Pasadena, Calif.: Worldwide Church of God, 1953.

──────. *Just What Do You Mean, Born Again?* Pasadena, Calif.: Worldwide Church of God, 1962.

──────. *The Missing Dimension in Sex.* Pasadena, Calif.: Worldwide Church of God, 1964.

──────. *Mystery of the Ages.* Pasadena, Calif.: Worldwide Church of God, 1985.

──────. *The Seven Laws of Success.* Pasadena, Calif.: Worldwide Church of God, 1974.

──────. *The United States and Britain in Prophecy.* Pasadena, Calif.: Worldwide Church of God, 1954.

──────. *Why Were You Born?* Pasadena, Calif.: Worldwide Church of God, 1957.

──────. *The Wonderful World of Tomorrow.* New York: Everest House, 1979.

Other WCG Sources

Bucher, J. F. L. *Armstrongism Bibliography.* Sydney, Australia: Author, 1983.

Hoeh, Herman L. *The True History of the True Church.* (Pasadena, Calif.: Worldwide Church of God, 1980.

The Plain Truth and *The Worldwide News.* Periodicals published for many years by the WCG.

Tkach, Joseph, Jr. *Transformed by Truth.* Sisters, Ore.: Multnomah Press, 1997.

Splinter Groups

Flurry, Gerald. *The Ezekiel Watchman.* Edmond, Okla.: Philadelphia Church of God, 1992.

──────. *Jeremiah: Prophet of Doom or Hope?* Edmond, Okla.: Philadelphia Church of God, 1993.

──────. *Lamentations and the End Time Laodiceans.* Edmond, Okla.: Philadelphia Church of God, 1993.

──────. *Malachi's Message.* Edmond, Okla.: Philadelphia Church of God, 1992.

Selected Splinter Group Periodicals

ACD Newsletter (Associated Churches).

The Philadelphia Trumpet (Philadelphia Church of God).

Prophecy Flash (Triumph Prophetic Ministries).

Twentieth Century Watch and *International News* (Church of God International).

Voice from Afar Newsletter (Twentieth Century Church of God, 1990).

Selected Secondary Sources

Benware, Paul N. *Ambassadors of Armstrongism.* Nutley, N.J.: Presbyterian & Reformed, 1975.

Campbell, Roger F. *Herbert W. Armstrong and His Worldwide Church of God.* Fort Washington, Penn.: Christian Literature Crusade, 1974.

DeLoach, Charles F. *The Armstrong Era.* Plainfield, N.J.: Logos International, 1971.

Hopkins, Joseph. *The Armstrong Empire.* Grand Rapids, Mich.: Eerdmanns, 1974.

Kirban, Salem. *Armstrong's Church of God.* Chicago: Moody Press, 1973.

Martin, Walter. *The Kingdom of the Cults.* Rev. ed. Minneapolis: Bethany House, 1985. (As of this writing, a new edition of Martin's classic is in the process of being published.)

————. *Martin Speaks Out on the Cults.* Ventura, Calif.: Vision House, 1983.

Mather, George, and Larry Nichols. *Dictionary of Cults, Sects, Religions and the Occult.* Grand Rapids, Mich.: Zondervan, 1993.

McNair, Marion. *Armstrongism: Religion or Rip-off?* Orlando, Fla.: Pacific-Charters, 1977.

Melton, J. Gordon. *The Encyclopedia of American Religions.* 2 vols. Wilmington, N.C.: McGrath, 1978; new 5th edition published in one volume, 1996.

————. *Encyclopedic Handbook of Cults in America.* New York: Garland, 1986.

Rader, Stanley R. *Against the Gates of Hell.* New York: Everest House, 1980.

Robinson, David. *Herbert Armstrong's Tangled Web.* Tulsa, Okla.: John Hadden, 1980.

Smith, Paul B. *Other Gospels.* Greenwood, S.C.: Attic, 1970.

Starkes, M. Thomas. *Confronting Popular Cults.* Nashville: Broadman, 1972.

————. *Confronting Cults Old and New.* Chatanooga, Tenn.: AMG Publishers, 1984.

Tuit, John. *The Truth Shall Make You Free*, Freehold Township, N.J.: Truth Foundation, 1981.

Selected Periodicals

"The Bible Reveals PLANE TRUTH." *Sower: The Bible Society in Australia, Inc.,* Winter 1996, p. 7.

Dean, Richard C. "Open Arms: Welcoming the Worldwide Church of God." *Religious Broadcasting,* February/March 1997, pp. 34-36, 38.

Gomes, Alan W. "The Worldwide Church of God: Acknowledging the 'Plain Truth' About the Trinity." *Christian Research Journal,* Spring/Summer 1994, pp. 29-31, 39-40.

Hopkins, Joseph. "Armstrong's Church of God: Mellowed Aberrations?" *Christianity Today,* April 15, 1977, pp. 22-24.

————. "Despite Scandals, Armstrong's Church Is Growing." *Christianity Today,*

August 6, 1982, pp. 48-49.

———. "Good Thinking! The Armstrong Family Business." *Eternity,* November 1977, pp. 58-61.

———. "What Is Satan's Fate?" *Tomorrow's World,* June 1977, pp. 7-9.

———. "Will Herbert W. Armstrong Rise Again?" *Christianity Today,* January 1988, p. 48.

LeBlanc, Doug. "The Worldwide Church of God: Resurrected into Orthodoxy." *Christian Research Journal,* Winter 1996, pp. 6-7, 44-48.

Pemente, Eric. "The Plain Truth About Herbert W. Armstrong." *Cornerstone* 11, no. 62 (n.d.): 14-17.

———. "When Christians Meet the Worldwide Church of God." *Christian Herald,* October 1988, p. 40.

Schweikert, Anahid. "Former Cult Embraces Bible Doctrines." *Charisma,* July 1996, p. 25.

Trott, Jon. "The Saga of a Cult Gone Good." *Cornerstone* 26, no. 3 (1997): 41-44.

Tucker, Ruth. "From the Fringe to the Fold: How the Worldwide Church of God Discovered the Plain Truth of the Gospel." *Christianity Today,* July 15, 1996, pp. 26-32.

Internet Addresses

Worldwide Church of God: http://www.wcg.org/pt/index.htm

Church of God International: info@cgi.org

Aarn, Philip: PAWFI@aol.com

Covington, David: Covin1d.aol.com

Covington, David (web site): http://members.aol.com/coving1d

Ferguson, William: quango@wavefront.com

Hutchinson, Janis: Jhutchinson@juno.com

Lain, Rodney: RLain@wavefront.com

Meyer, William: am.d.meyer@postoffice.worldnet.att.net

Tabladillo, Mark (web site): quango.net/tabladillo/wcgweb2.html